How
Schools
Shortchange
Girls

—The AAUW Report

How
Schools
Shortchange
Girls

—THE AAUW REPORT

◆

A Study of Major Findings on
Girls and Education

◆

*Commissioned by the AAUW Educational Foundation
and researched by the Wellesley College
Center for Research on Women*

MARLOWE & COMPANY

NEW YORK

First trade paperback edition, 1995

Published in the United States by
Marlowe & Company
632 Broadway, Seventh Floor
New York, New York 10012

Copyright © 1992 American Association of University Women Educational Foundation

All rights reserved. No part of this book may be reproduced, in any form, without written
permission from the publishers, unless by a reviewer who wishes to quote brief passages.

Library of Congress Cataloging-in-Publication Data

How schools shortchange girls.

1. Women—Education—United States. 2. Educational
equalization—United States. I. Wellesley College
Center for Research on Women. II. American
Association of University Women Educational
Foundation.
LC1752.H68 1992   370.19'345   91-44287

ISBN 1-56924-821-4

TABLE OF CONTENTS

◆

ACKNOWLEDGMENTS

♦

This report was prepared by the Wellesley College Center for Research on Women under a contract from the American Association of University Women Educational Foundation. From its inception, the report has been a team effort. Susan McGee Bailey, Center Director, served as project director and principal author. In addition to researching and writing major sections of the report, core team members Lynn C. Burbridge, Patricia B. Campbell, Barbara L. Jackson, Fern Marx, and Peggy McIntosh discussed, reviewed, and debated every aspect of the project for its entire twelve-month life. Janice Earle, David and Myra Sadker, Margaret Stubbs, and Gretchen Wilbur contributed reviews of the research literature in specific areas. Holly Knox conducted interviews with key policymakers, and Judy Logan and Cathy Nelson interviewed classroom teachers and school administrators.

Authors for Part One were Susan Bailey, Lynn Burbridge, and Barbara Jackson; for Part Two, Lynn Burbridge, Patricia Campbell, Susan Bailey, and Fern Marx; for Part Three, Patricia Campbell and Susan Bailey; for Part Four, Susan Bailey, Peggy McIntosh, David and Myra Sadker, Janice Earle, Margaret Stubbs, and Gretchen Wilbur. Appendix A was compiled by Barbara Jackson.

The project was strengthened by collaboration with the State Assessment Center at the Council of Chief State School Officers and with the National Association of State Boards of Education. Ramsey Selden, Barbara Clements, and Rolf Blank at the State Assessment Center wrote the appendix "The Condition of Indicators on Gender Equity."

Colleagues at the Wellesley College Center for Research on Women, the

American Association of University Women, and at universities, research centers, policy offices, state and federal education agencies, and public schools around the country contributed important data, valuable insights, and unfailing good humor. Jan Putnam commented on drafts throughout the project. Margaret Dunkle, former director of the AAUW Educational Foundation, provided guidance for many months and Priscilla Little of the Foundation was a model of patience and energy. AAUW Managing Editor Sheila Buckmaster shepherded the manuscript through many versions. Esther Diamond, Sumru Erkut, Annie Rogers, and Emily Style commented on sections of the report. The Research Advisory Committee of the AAUW Educational Foundation, made up of Maggie Ford, Connie Gipson, Jane Kahle, Dagmar McGill, and Annie Rogers, contributed important insights and information at several critical points.

The report would have been impossible without the dedication of tireless undergraduate assistants, Gitana Garofalo, Leo Garofalo, Christine Jacobson, Erin Tracy, and Amy Symons, as well as the superb work of two graduate assistants, Michele Guyton and Tracy Tsugawa. Pam Baker, Molly Jones, and Faye Stylianopoules typed endless drafts, attended to bibliographic format, and kept us all sane. At the Wellesley College Clapp Library, Karen Jensen in the Interlibrary Loan Office and Reference Librarian Joan Campbell found articles, books, and statistics with speed and generosity.

FOREWORD

♦

In the midst of national education-reform efforts earlier in this decade it became disturbingly apparent to members of the American Association of University Women that girls were not adequately represented or addressed in the wide-ranging discussions and debates taking place throughout the country. Girls, in fact, were nearly invisible.

We knew, based on the work of Carol Gilligan, Myra and David Sadker, and others, that many girls undergo an erosion of self-esteem during adolescence. Studies indicate that most girls in first grade have skills and ambitions comparable to those of boys, whereas girls finishing high school have disproportionately less confidence in their academic abilities than do boys. We wanted to know why—and what role schooling plays in this gap.

Before we could add our voice in a meaningful way, we needed a comprehensive understanding of the educational experiences of America's girls and boys. How are girls faring in our nation's schools? How are they doing in contrast to boys? What happens in the classroom? Is education really equitable?

These fundamental yet challenging questions led the AAUW Educational Foundation to explore what girls experience in school, from the first days of kindergarten to the closing days of high school. In the early 1990s we launched an investigation to find out as much as we could about how girls are taught and how they learn in America's public schools. We issued a request for proposals for a thorough literature review on the subject of girls and education. After reviewing proposals from researchers around the country, the AAUW Educational Foundation board commissioned the Wellesley

College Center for Research on Women to analyze and synthesize reports and studies documenting the experiences, behaviors, courses of study and learning environments of girls in school.

How Schools Shortchange Girls — The AAUW Report is the result of this groundbreaking project. The report reflects more than that 1,300 studies and is credited with drawing national attention to the disturbing evidence that girls are not receiving the same quality, or even quantity, of education as their brothers. By stereotyping women's roles, popular culture plays a role in shortchanging girls by limiting their horizons and expectations. Unintentionally, schools sometimes follow suit, depriving girls of classroom attention, ignoring the value of cooperative learning, and presenting texts and lessons in which female role models are conspicuously absent.

How Schools Shortchange Girls — The AAUW Report explores issues that are often hidden from view and highlights a problem of national proportions and consequence. This book not only addresses the problems but offers the groundwork for solutions, outlining recommendations to help ensure that girls and boys are both encouraged—and given the tools—to maximize their potential.

For more than a century AAUW has tackled tough education end equity issues by studying, then acting. AAUW's first national study, undertaken in 1885, provided sufficient evidence to dispel the popular myth that higher education was harmful to a woman's health. In the 1990's *How Schools Shortchange Girls — The AAUW Report* show us how girls—tomorrow's women—are faring during their formative school experiences.

A well-reasoned call to action, this book underscores the necessity of shared responsibility for the education of our nation's youth. The information presented here is spawning a heightened sensitivity to the needs of girls. The Ms. Foundation, for example, credits AAUW's research and the work of Carol Gilligan and others for helping to inspire its national "Take Our Daughters to Work" Day. Gender equity provisions written into Goals 2000: Educate America and the Elementary and Secondary Education Act, both passed in 1994, likewise were influenced by AAUW's seminal research.

What is needed to further the futures of our children and our country? Concerted awareness and action on the part of students, parents, teachers, and administrators will enable us to provide the best education possible for all girls and boys. We need to help each and every student reach beyond stereotypes to learn the critical-thinking and problem-solving skills so crucial in our increasingly complex and demanding world.

Our country cannot afford to have half its students shortchanged in school. By the year 2005, women will make up 48 percent of our work force. To remain competitive in the global economy, we need to build the skills of all our children. If we shortchange girls, we shortchange America.

Alice Ann Leidel
President
AAUW Educational Foundation
March 1995

PART

FRAMING
THE ISSUES:
AN
INTRODUCTION

WHY A REPORT ON GIRLS?

♦

The absence of attention to girls in the current education debate suggests that girls and boys have identical educational experiences in school. Nothing could be further from the truth. Whether one looks at achievement scores, curriculum design, self-esteem levels, or staffing patterns, it is clear that sex and gender make a difference in the nation's public elementary and secondary schools. There is clear evidence that the educational system is not meeting girls' needs. Girls and boys enter school roughly equal in measured ability. On some measures of school readiness, such as fine motor control, girls are ahead of boys. Twelve years later, girls have fallen behind their male classmates in key areas such as higher-level mathematics and measures of self-esteem.

But rather than acknowledging and exploring the links among sex, gender, and academic performance, the current debate ignores them. Report after report refers to "students"

> "**W**e take for granted that our schools are communities, when, in fact, they are merely institutions that can become communities only when we work at it. But, with proper attention to all the individuals within the school, we can create an experience for students that demonstrates what it means to be a compassionate, involved citizen. For it is only within a community, not an institution, that we learn how to hold fast to such principles as working for the common good, empathy, equity, and self-respect."
>
> George H. Wood,.
> "Teaching for Democracy,"
> *Educational Leadership*,
> November 1990, p.33.

or "youth" or "eighth-graders"—sex unspecified. This lack of specificity perpetuates the invisibility of girls and compromises the education of our nation's students. By ignoring the strengths and contributions as well as the educational needs of girls, the current debate is short-changing not only our daughters but our sons as well. Serious consideration of girls is not merely a matter of justice; it is an issue of economic survival and basic common sense. Today's students are tomorrow's citizens, parents, and workers. It is they who will bear the responsibility for maintaining a vital and creative society. To leave girls on the sidelines in discussions of educational reform is to deprive ourselves of the full potential of half of our work force, half of our citizenry, and half of the parents of the next generation.

Furthermore, when we ignore girls, we lose sight of critical aspects of social development that our culture has traditionally assigned to women but that are equally important for men. Schools must help girls *and* boys acquire both the relational and the competitive skills needed for full participation in the work force, family, and community.

Education in the United States has long given lip service to the development of individual potential and a concern for equity, but attention has focused primarily on the preparation of future workers. By maintaining this emphasis, the current school-reform movement risks losing sight of the fuller American dream—a dream that sees excellence not just in terms of products but also in terms of people and their opportunities and choices. It is a dream of a nation in which individuals believe in and belong to a larger community. By studying what happens to girls in school, we can gain valuable insights about what has to change in order for each student—every girl and every boy—to do as well as she or he can. Our children—and our nation—deserve nothing less.

This report documents the ways in which the public school system shortchanges girls. It is based on research on the accomplishments, behaviors, and needs of girls from preschool through high school. Included in the report are recommendations to improve education for both girls and boys and help prepare them for the next century. Implicit in these recommendations is a vision of schools and students as integral parts of wider communities. Thus, the report is grounded in an understanding of schools *in* communities as well as in a vision of schools *as* communities.

Notes on Terminology

The terms *sex* and *gender* are often used interchangeably. In this report, we have tried to use *sex* only when referring to individuals as biologically female or male, and *gender* when also referring to different sets of expectations and limitations imposed by society on girls and boys simply because they are female or male. Despite our attempts to maintain these distinctions, the report reviews research by many authors, and our usage usually conforms to that of the research we report.

Designations for racial and ethnic groups are in a constant state of evolution. Until recently *black* was the accepted term for members of the United States population who are of African descent. *African American* is now becoming more common. *Hispanic* has been used to denote Spanish-speaking members of the population, but there has been an increasing use of *Latina* and *Latino* instead. The indigenous people of the United States are referred to both as *Native Americans* and as *American Indians*.

Further, some of these groups are quite heterogeneous. For example, the common term *Latina* can refer to women and girls who trace their ancestry to Mexico, Cuba, Puerto Rico, and other Central American, South American, and Caribbean regions. The term *Asian American* incorporates Vietnamese Americans, Chinese Americans, Japanese Americans, Pakistani Americans, and so on. Unfortunately, data limitations and gaps in the literature rarely permit examination of such differences within broadly labeled groups.

Moreover, all of these groups are often lumped together in one category, referred to as *ethnic minorities* or *nonwhites*. Thus the tremendous diversity in the country is often misrepresented as a simple contrast between "majority whites" and "minority nonwhites."

We have attempted to be sensitive to changes in racial terminology and the differences among and between various ethnic groups, but we have encountered many limitations. First, there is no general agreement on what is or is not the "best designation" for various groups. Second, since this document provides an extensive review of the literature, we have felt obligated to use the terms used by authors quoted or cited. Third, economy in presentation has often required the use of more general terms, in spite of the diversity that is glossed over in the process. Every effort has been taken to ensure that the term used is appropriate and makes sense within its context.

EDUCATING THE NEW WORK FORCE

What a student learns—or does not learn—in school has lasting effects. No discussion of girls' education can ignore the reality of women's lives. Women make up 45 percent of the nation's work force, and this percentage is increasing.[1] But women are heavily concentrated in a narrow range of occupations traditionally considered appropriate for them. Sixty percent of all women working outside the home are working in clerical, service, or professional positions, and more than 60 percent of these professional women are in female-intensive fields such as school teaching and nursing.[2] Occupational segregation among women of color is even more extreme. Forty-one percent of black women working in service occupations are employed as chambermaids, welfare service aides, cleaners, or nurse's aides.[3] For Hispanic women, job segregation has meant disproportionate employment in low-level factory jobs in some of the industries hardest hit by the current downturn in the economy.[4]

WOMEN'S WAGES. Given their extreme occupational segregation, it is not surprising that women's wages are lower than men's wages. This holds true even when years of education are the same, and when the comparison is between full-time, year-round workers. Women with eight or fewer years of education earn only 66 percent of the wages of similarly educated men; even women with five or more years of college make only 69 cents for every dollar earned by their male colleagues with an equal number of years of education.[5]

Job segregation is not the only factor influencing women's lower earnings. Women earn less than men even when they hold identical jobs. Female machine operators, secretaries, lawyers, and uni-

(continued from previous page)

versity professors all make less than their male colleagues.[6]

But the subjects that women study in school make a difference. Wage differentials favoring men are considerably less—or disappear altogether—for women in their early thirties who have earned eight or more mathematics credits in college.[7] *To study college-level mathematics, however, students must have taken high school courses and believe that mathematics is for them, not only for others.*

IMPORTANCE OF WOMEN'S EDUCATION TO FAMILY INCOME. *Between 1975 and 1985 wage growth slowed dramatically for men and women. Because of the dip in men's wages, the earnings of women have come to represent an increasing proportion of family income. A wife's earnings now constitute 50 percent of black family income, 40 percent of Hispanic family income, and 35 percent of white family income. Married couples in which both husband and wife are employed have the highest incomes, and it is only among this group that the earnings of black and Hispanic families even approach the earnings of white families.*[8]

The families most in danger of poverty are those headed by women, particularly women of color. Since women's wages are lower than men's and single-parent families do not benefit from two incomes, child poverty rates are high in female-headed households; among whites the rate is 47 percent and among blacks it is 72 percent.[9]

Higher levels of education among mothers play an important role in reducing poverty among children. Childhood poverty is almost inescapable in single-parent families headed by women without high school diplomas: the rate is 87 percent for blacks and 77 percent for whites.[10] *Inadequate education not only lowers opportunities for women, but jeopardizes their children as well. Given the increase in the number and percentage of women who are single parents and the growing importance of women's wages to total family income, the education of women is important not only for women as individuals, but also for women as mothers, as family members, and as effective and creative citizens of larger communities.*

---

[1] H. Fullerton, Jr., "New Labor Force Projections Spanning 1988 to 2000," *Monthly Labor Review* 112 (November 1989): 2, Table 1.

[2] C. Taeuber, ed. *Statistical Handbook on Women in America* (Phoenix: Oryx Press, 1991), p. 128, Table B5-1.

[3] J. Malveaux, "The Economic Status of Black Families," in H. McAdoo, ed., *Black Families* (Newbury Park: Sage Publications, 1988).

[4] M. Escutia and M. Prieto, *Hispanics in the Workforce, Part II: Hispanic Women* (Washington. DC: National Council of La Raza, Policy Analysis Center, Office of Research, Advocacy, and Legislation, 1988).

[5] U.S. Department of Education, Office of Educational Research and Improvement, *Digest of Education Statistics,* 1990, p. 363, Table 344.

[6] U.S. Department of Commerce, Bureau of the Census. *Statistical Abstract of the United States: 1990,* 110th ed. (Washington, DC: U.S. Government Printing Office, 1990), p. 409, Table 671.

[7] C. Adelman, *Women at Thirtysomething: Paradoxes of Attainment* (Washington, DC: U.S. Department of Education, 1991), p. 24.

[8] U.S. Department of Commerce, Bureau of the Census. *Statistical Abstract of the United States: 1990,* p. 451, Table 729.

[9] U.S. Congress, House, Committee on Ways and Means. *Overview of Entitlement Programs: 1990 Green Book* (Washington, DC: U.S. Government Printing Office, 1990), p. 956, Table 56.

[10] Ibid.

THE ABSENCE OF GIRLS IN THE CURRENT DEBATE ON EDUCATION

♦

Sixty percent of the education-reform-report commissions reviewed for this study had less than 30 percent female representation. Only two were at least 50 percent female.

In 1983, the U.S. Department of Education published *A Nation at Risk*, sparking school-reform efforts across the country. Educational commissions, committees, and special studies were quickly assembled and funded by a wide range of organizations, foundations, and government agencies. Many of their findings have since been published. Thirty-five reports issued by special task forces and commissions were reviewed for this study to assess the amount of attention given to gender and sex equity issues.[1] The review addressed four questions:

♦ To what degree did women participate as members or hold leadership positions on the special task forces or commissions?

♦ Did the issues or concerns that prompted a particular report include gender or sex equity?

♦ Did the data, the rationale, or background information presented include sex or gender as a separate category?

♦ Did the recommendations specifically address gender issues?

Few women held leadership positions on the thirty-five commissions, task forces, or boards of directors studied.[2] Although women were members of all the groups except one, their percentage varied greatly; only two groups had at least 50 percent female representation.[3] Most of the reports do not define the educational issues under review in terms of gender, nor do they include sex as a separate category in their data analyses and background information. Few of the recommendations are framed with sex or gender in mind. The majority of the reports imply that the only significant problems girls may face are getting pregnant at an early age, dropping out of school, and thereby increasing the number of female-headed households living in poverty. While these are incontestable problems, the concentration on these issues to the exclusion of others leads to strategies directed toward individual rather than systemic change and programs focused on girls' personal decisions rather than policy initiatives to improve the educational system.

Four of the reports include gender as a category in defining the students seen at risk and/or the issues under consideration.[4] One of these reports was published by the National Board of Inquiry, convened by the National Coalition of Advocates for Students (NCAS); this board was one of the few co-chaired by a woman. The NCAS report, *Barriers to Excellence: Our Children at Risk* (1985), defined its focus this way:

> *"Who are the children at risk? They include a large proportion of young people from poor families of all races. They include minority and immigrant children who face discriminatory policies and practices, large numbers of girls and young women who miss out on education opportunities routinely afforded males, and children with special needs who are unserved,*

underserved, or improperly categorized because of handicap or learning difficulties."[5]

The NCAS rationale and background statement specifically mention race, class, culture, and sex. The report suggests that teen pregnancy may be directly linked to poor achievement and low educational aspirations. It is also the only report of the thirty-five reviewed to directly address Title IX of the Education Amendments of 1972, prohibiting sex discrimination in education programs receiving federal funds. The report urges, "Renew commitment to Title IX, thereby assuring that female students will have an opportunity to develop their talents and skills fully."[6]

Title IX

Under Title IX of the Education Amendments of 1972, discrimination on the basis of sex is illegal in any educational program receiving federal funding. Federal enforcement of Title IX is complaint-driven, and over the past decade the U.S. Office of Civil Rights has not actively pursued Title IX enforcement. In 1990, researchers who spent six months visiting twenty-five rural school districts in twenty-one states reported that 37 percent of the district administrators they interviewed saw no Title IX compliance issues in their districts. Some of these administrators expressed the view that it was "stupid" or "frivolous" to worry about equal opportunities for girls and boys. Furthermore, the research team reported that in some of the school districts where the administration perceived no problems, Title IX violations appeared to exist in terms of athletic

NEEDED:
WOMEN IN THE LEADERSHIP OF PUBLIC EDUCATION
···

SCHOOL BOARDS. *In 1927, 10.2 percent of all local school board members were female. By 1990 that percentage had risen to only 33.7. Minority constituencies are even more severely underrepresented. Only 2.9 percent of school board members are black and only 1.3 percent are Hispanic. The data are not reported by sex within racial categories.*

TEACHERS AND ADMINISTRATORS. *Policies of local boards of education are implemented by the superintendent of schools and central office staff. Despite the fact that public elementary and secondary education is still considered a "woman's field"— 72 percent of all elementary and secondary school teachers are female—women hold few of the upper management positions in our public schools (see graph).*

CHIEF STATE SCHOOL OFFICERS. *The chief state school officer in each state provides leadership and direc-*

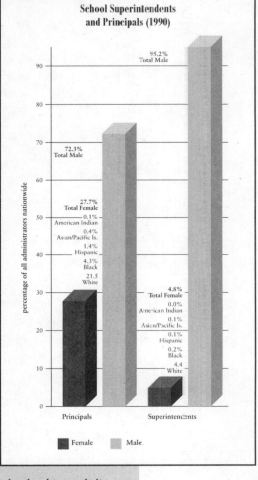

School Superintendents and Principals (1990)

percentage of all administrators nationwide

Principals

72.3% Total Male

27.7% Total Female
0.1% American Indian
0.4% Asian/Pacific Is.
1.4% Hispanic
4.3% Black
21.5 White

Superintendents

95.2% Total Male

4.8% Total Female
0.0% American Indian
0.1% Asian/Pacific Is.
0.1% Hispanic
0.2% Black
4.4 White

■ Female   ■ Male

(continued from previous page)

tion for the state public school system. In 1991, only nine of the fifty chief state school officers were women—the largest number in recent years.

The method of selecting chief state school officers varies from state to state; in eighteen states they are elected by popular vote, in twenty-seven they are appointed by the state board of education, and in five they are appointed by the governor. Eight of the nine women heading state education agencies in 1991 were elected by popular vote; one was appointed by a governor.

Graph excludes states that do not report data by sex and race. Source: *Women and Minorities in School Administration: Facts and Figures 1989–90.* American Association of School Administrators, pp. 4, 5, 8, 9, 14, 20.

opportunities and sex segregation in higher level mathematics and science classes. An additional 28 percent of the district administrators interviewed replied that they believed their districts were within the letter of the law but that they had not gone beyond equal access. A third group, 35 percent of the sample, reported that they were concerned that equal access in the narrow sense was not sufficient to provide genuine equal opportunity for girls and boys. Administrators in this latter group had been faced with sex discrimination suits and/or had attended equity workshops.[7]

This research indicates that sex and gender equity issues are still not well understood by many educators. The research also suggests that in-service training on equity issues can both increase awareness and provide specific tools for achieving a more equitable educational environment. Renewed attention to the vigorous enforcement of Title IX must be a top priority for everyone concerned with the quality of public education in the United States.

The National Education Goals

Education has remained on the national agenda ever since the 1983 publication of *A Nation at Risk*. In February 1990, President Bush and the National Governors Association set a series of ambitious education goals to be met by the year 2000.[8] Setting goals is one thing; reaching them is another. Educators across the nation are faced with the task of developing programs that will remedy in a decade all that we have not managed to accomplish in the last century.

In 1991 the President and the Department of Education presented *America 2000* as a "plan to move every community in America toward these goals."[9] None of the strategies proposed in *America 2000* is gender specific. Girls are once again ignored in setting the national agenda.

The National Coalition for Women and Girls in Education has repeatedly noted that the National Education Goals cannot be met without specific attention to girls.[10] Solutions designed to meet everyone's needs risk meeting no one's. Attention must be directed to those characteristics that differentiate girls from boys as well as to the differences found among girls of various racial, ethnic, socioeconomic, and cultural groups. Thus *The AAUW Report* focuses—to the extent the data allow—both on the things girls share as well as on their differences.

THE DEVELOPMENT OF GENDER ROLES: AN OVERVIEW

♦

From pink and blue tags in hospital nurseries, to Barbie dolls and G.I. Joes, and on to cheerleaders and football players, our society holds different expectations for girls and boys. These expectations in turn generate different patterns of behavior toward children, depending on their sex.*

> "Sex differences most consistently seem to be the result of social factors. This includes both the different socialization experiences that males and females have and the socially determined assumptions and viewpoints of researchers studying the area."
>
> M. Harway and L. Moss, "Sex Differences: The Evidence from Biology" in *Social and Cognitive Skills*, edited by M. Liss [New York: Academic Press, 1983], p. 40.

The Early Years

Although the causes are debated, most research indicates that children aged two to three use the terms "boy" and "girl" as simple labels rather than as conceptual categories.[11] By age four, societal training in seeing the sexes as "opposite" has taken hold and children begin to think of girls and "girls' things" as the opposite of boys and "boys' things," but they do not yet feel a sense of necessity about what people of each sex must do. At four or five years old, they may try

It is important to recognize that the research consists primarily of studies on white middle-class girls and boys. The effects of race, ethnicity, and socioeconomic class on gender development have not been studied adequately.

to enforce certain sex roles for other children, but this is usually as much a matter of reaching their own objectives as it is a matter of belief in "rules."[12] There is evidence that boys are more rigidly committed to sex roles than girls are. Boys more consistently choose and prefer sex-typed toys and activities, and these preferences accelerate with age throughout early childhood.[13]

By the time they are six or seven, children have clear ideas about gender, based on what they see in the world around them, and both girls and boys strive for conformity with gender-stereotyped roles.[14] Both sexes strongly prefer sex-segregated play groups at this age.[15]

Children aged eight to ten are more flexible regarding occupational roles for women and men, and there is some reduction of sex-segregated behavior.[16] However, most children continue to prefer to spend time with same-sex friends.[17]

Girls and boys in elementary school are equally likely to report feelings of sadness, self-derogation, and physical complaints. However, boys report more problems with behavior and relationships with other children.[18] Other research notes that young boys report feelings of anger and hostility more frequently than do young girls.[19] Further study of the strengths of elementary school girls is needed, particularly in view of the higher rates of depression among older, adolescent girls.[20]

Early Adolescence

In early adolescence the relative flexibility surrounding appropriate behavior for each sex observed among eight-to-ten-year-olds lessens and more rigid adherence to gender roles becomes the norm. "Girls become more unwilling to admit that they ever do act like boys. Boys are never very willing to admit acting like girls. . . "[21]

"**F**airly distinctive styles of interaction develop in all-boy and all-girl groups. Thus, the segregated play groups constitute powerful socialization environments in which children acquire distinctive interaction skills that are adapted to same-sex partners...the distinctive patterns developed by the two sexes at this time have implications for the same-sex and cross-sex relationships that individuals form as they enter adolescence and adulthood."

Eleanor Maccoby, "Gender and Relationships," *American Psychologist* 45 {April 1990}, p. 516.

Early adolescence is a significant transition period for both sexes, but research reveals it to be a particularly difficult time for girls. Moving from "young girl" to "young woman" involves meeting unique demands in a culture that both idealizes and exploits the sexuality of young women while assigning them roles that are clearly less valued than male roles. For girls, the onset of menstruation serves as a specific marker of bodily changes. While the average age of first menstruation in the United States is 12.8 years, the age range is wide, from as early as 10 to as late as 16.[22] On average, the pubertal period is ending for girls just as it is beginning for boys. At age 11 or 12, differences between boys and girls are particularly striking.

"By age 11, the vast majority of girls have entered the pubertal period for height growth...By contrast, virtually none of the boys have reached the onset of the pubertal period...By 12 years of age still less than one-fourth of the boys have entered the pubertal period."[23]

For girls who are early maturers, puberty can be a particularly trying time. They tend to be heavier than their classmates in a culture that values slimness, and their social and emotional development may not match their physically mature appearance.[24] Early-maturing girls exhibit more eating problems than average or late maturers and are at greater risk for depression.[25]

Being liked by others of their own sex matters more to adolescent girls than it does to boys.[26] In fact, as girls grow up and move into adolescence there is a steady increase in the degree of intimacy they report in their friendships with other girls. This pattern is not true for boys.[27] Girls in grades six and seven rate being popular and well-liked as more important than being perceived as competent or independent. Boys, on the other hand, are more likely to rank independence and competence as important.[28]

Large-scale empirical studies, public-opinion polls, and in-depth clinical studies following individual girls through school all report significant declines in girls' self-esteem and self-confidence as they move from childhood to early adolescence, at least among the white middle-class girls most often studied.[29] A nationwide survey commissioned by the American Association of University Women (AAUW) in 1990 found that on average 69 percent of elementary school boys and 60 percent of elementary school girls reported that they were "happy the way I am"; among high school students the percentages were 46 percent for boys and only 29 percent for girls.[30]

The AAUW survey revealed sharp differences in self-esteem among girls from different racial and ethnic groups. Among elementary school girls, 55 percent of white girls, 65 percent of black girls, and 68 percent of Hispanic girls reported being "happy as I am." But in high school, agreement with the statement came from

THE SILENCE OF GIRLS

Carol Gilligan, Lyn Mikel Brown, and Annie Rogers at the Harvard Project on the Psychology of Women and the Development of Girls write eloquently about the silencing of girls as they move from the elementary grades into junior high and high school. Rogers and Gilligan report that young girls show

> striking capacities for self-confidence, courage and resistance to harmful norms of feminine behavior as well as a detailed and complex knowledge of the human social world....Up until the age of eleven or twelve...girls are quite clear and candid about what they think and feel and know.[1]

But as girls mature and enter mid-adolescence, their voices become more tentative and conflicted. Their responses reveal a sometimes debilitating tension between caring for themselves and caring for others, between their understanding of the world and their awareness that it is not appropriate to speak or act on this understanding.

While much of the work of the Harvard Project in the past has been with predominantly white upper-middle-class students, many studying in private all-girls' schools, the very selectivity of their sample raises compelling questions.[2] If young women of relative privilege, studying in environments designed to foster their education and development, exhibit increasingly conflicted views of themselves and their responsibilities and opportunities in the world, what does this reveal about the cultural norms these schools, and perhaps all schools, are reinforcing for young women?

---

[1] A. Rogers and C. Gilligan, "Translating Girls' Voices: Two

Languages of Development," Harvard University Graduate School of Education, Harvard Project on the Psychology of Women and the Development of Girls, 1988, pp. 42–43.

[2] Current project work includes girls in public-school settings and girls from various racial, ethnic, and socioeconomic backgrounds.

only 22 percent of the white girls and 30 percent of the Hispanic girls, compared to 58 percent of the black girls.[31] However, these black girls did not have high levels of self-esteem in areas related to school. Further evidence of low levels of confidence in academic areas among black girls is presented later in this report. Obviously, self-esteem is a complex construct, and further study of the various strengths and perspectives of girls from many different backgrounds is needed in order to design educational programs that can benefit all girls.

The type of school, whether K–8, middle school, or junior high school, and the timing of the transition from one school to another is particularly important for girls. Research reveals that girls' self-esteem benefits if there is only one transition at the end of eighth grade rather than the two changes: first from elementary school to middle or junior high school and, second, from there to high school.

"In terms of self-esteem the K–6/JH/SH girls never recover from the seventh-grade drop in self-esteem...they respond more, not less, negatively to the transition into senior high school than does the cohort who has to make only one change at a more mature age."[32]

The patterns of declining self-esteem, negative body image, and depression that begin at early adolescence do not disappear as girls mature. Recent research traces depression in twelfth grade to changes experienced earlier in adolescence and to the coping strategies individuals develop to deal with stressful events.[33]

Furthermore, young women in high school confront even more directly the conflicting expectations for women in our society.

> *"...the growing inconsistencies and contradictions of female adolescence provide greater stress and fewer coping resources for girls....It appears that current cohorts of girls experience stress because of conflicting demands to achieve in the public sphere and be successful in interpersonal relations, especially dating."*[34]

Marriage, family, and employment outside the home are not equal situations for women and men in our society. Teenage girls know this. It is a discouraging reality, a reality that schools alone cannot change, but one that will not change until schooling changes.

PART 2

GIRLS
IN
SCHOOL

Part Two reviews data on the achievement and participation of girls in public school programs from preschool through the senior year of high school.

Research belies the common assumption that early education environments are better for girls than for boys. Educators must turn their attention to developing curricula that meet the developmental needs of girls as well as boys. Recognizing those needs is the first step. At present, for example, girls are identified much less frequently than boys as candidates for special education.

Despite a narrowing of the "gender gaps" in verbal and mathematical performance, girls are not doing as well as boys in our nation's schools. The physical sciences is one critical area in which girls continue to trail behind boys. More discouraging still, even girls who take the same mathematics and science courses as boys and perform equally well on tests are much less apt to pursue scientific or technological careers than are their male classmates. This is a "gender gap" our nation can no longer afford to ignore.

Research on sex, race, ethnicity, and socioeconomic status suggests that girls of low socioeconomic status have better test scores than boys of like background in the lower grades, but that by high school this advantage has disappeared. Furthermore, among students of high socioeconomic status, boys from all racial and ethnic groups have better test scores than girls. Nevertheless,

"The belief in the critical consequences of the early childhood years for subsequent development is one of the most universally cherished psychological insights of the twentieth century."

S. Greenberg, "Educational Equity in Early Childhood Environments," in *Handbook for Achieving Sex Equity through Education,* ed. Susan S. Klein (Baltimore: Johns Hopkins University Press, 1985), p. 457.

girls generally receive better grades than boys, regardless of race or socioeconomic status.

Research documents that the vocational education system has not succeeded in eliminating sex-segregated course-taking patterns, in part because relatively few resources have been devoted to sex-equity programs. The passage of the 1990 vocational education amendments offers an opportunity for change, but it is too soon to tell how much change it will bring. Certainly no change will take place without the combined efforts of vocational educators and community members.

Another fallacy is the commonly held belief that pregnancy accounts for most female school dropouts. Not so. More than half the girls who leave school before receiving a high school diploma do so for other reasons. In fact, girls, like boys, often drop out because school becomes irrelevant to their lives. In any case, discrimination against pregnant teens and teenage mothers is still common in schools across the country, despite the fact that such treatment has been illegal since the passage of Title IX of the Education Amendments in 1972.

Title IX also prohibits discrimination in sports programs, and the participation of girls in interscholastic athletics has increased dramatically since the early 1970s. However, boys' participation is still almost double that of girls.

The research reported here provides both a solid basis and a strong rationale for renewed efforts on behalf of girls in the nation's schools.

CHAPTER ONE

YOUNG GIRLS:
THE PRESCHOOL EXPERIENCE
♦

In 1989 the U.S. Census Bureau reported that 55 percent of all three-to-five-year-olds attended preprimary programs, at least for a portion of the day.[1] Preprimary programs are not mandatory and parents can choose whether or not to send their children. No data are available on enrollment in these programs by sex, so the assumption that enrollments of girls and boys are fairly equal remains uncontested. What we do know is that nondisabled low-income children are less than half as likely as higher-income children to receive prekindergarten schooling, despite the availability of the federal Headstart program since the mid-1960s.

Gender Equity Issues in Early Education Environments

By the time children of three or older enter a child-care or preschool setting, they already have experiences and skills that influence their perceptions and actions. In a discussion of sex equity in early-childhood education environments, Selma Greenberg of Hofstra University notes that young girls and boys have often acquired different skills and thus have different educational needs.[2]

There is a commonly held myth that early-education environments meet the needs of girls better than boys.[3]

"**P**reschool boys handle more tools, throw more balls, construct more Lego bridges, build more block towers, and tinker more with simple mechanical objects than do girls."

J. Kahle, "Why Girls Don't Know," in *What Research Says to the Science Teacher— The Process of Knowing*, ed. M. Rowe (Washington, DC: National Science Teachers Association, 1990), 6:55–67.

But rather than being better for girls, it would appear that many schools engage girls in activities in which they are already more proficient than are young boys. The traditional working assumption at the preschool level is that children need impulse-control training, small-muscle development, and language enhancement to be successful in their early years in school. Since many girls tend to achieve competency in these areas before they arrive in group settings, teachers turn their attention toward boys, whose development in these areas lags behind that of girls.[4] Indeed, one study of children from educationally advantaged homes found that preschool experience reduced sex differences in language achievement scores between girls and boys—by raising boys' scores.[5]

Many activities chosen by young boys, such as large-motor activities and investigatory and experimental activities, are considered "free play" and are not part of the regular, structured curriculum. If young girls are not specifically encouraged to participate in these "boy" activities, they do not receive a full and balanced set of educational experiences. Few of us choose to spend time in activities where we do not feel comfortable or competent.

During the past three decades, there has been significant development and diversification in early-childhood education programs, but there have been few carefully controlled studies of the varying effects of particular preschool environments on girls and boys.[6] However, some intriguing findings have been reported. When boys and girls who participated in Headstart programs using four different types of preschool curricula were

SPECIAL EDUCATION

Boys *outnumber girls in special-education programs by startling percentages. However, research on special education has rarely focused on gender issues.*

The graph at right shows that more than two-thirds of all students in special-education programs are male. In fact, the more "subjective" the diagnosis, the higher the representation of boys.

One traditional explanation for the disproportionate number of boys in special-education programs is that males are born more often with disabling conditions. However, a careful examination of the existing data does not fully support this explanation.

Several recent research studies raise new questions about the identification of

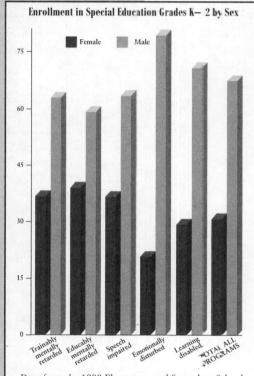

Enrollment in Special Education Grades K– 2 by Sex

Data from the 1988 Elementary and Secondary School Civil Rights Survey. U.S. Department of Education, Office of Civil Rights.

students with special needs. Medical reports on learning disabilities and attention-deficit disorders indicate that they occur almost equally in boys and girls. However, schools regularly identify many more boys than girls in these areas. Furthermore, a recent review of research data indicates that girls who are identified as learning-disabled by school personnel have lower IQs than do boys who are referred to special-education classes.[1] Rather than identifying learning problems, school personnel may be mislabeling behavioral problems.[2] Girls who sit quietly are ignored; boys who act out are placed in special programs that may not meet their needs.

Boys who are enrolled inappropriately in special-education classes face limited educational opportunities and carry a lifelong label. Girls with special needs who are not placed in special-education classes are deprived of the specialized services they need to develop fully.

Once students are placed in special-education programs, they often are exposed to curricular offerings that are heavily stereotyped in terms of gender roles.[3] The irony is that students whose options are already limited by physical and developmental disabilities need more, not fewer, degrees of freedom in terms of occupational and personal choices. This is particularly true for girls with disabilities who must contend not only with their disabling condition, but with the limitations our society places on women.

Given the composition of the population, enrollment data in special education also reveal a disproportionately high number of minority students in classes for the mentally retarded. However, data are not available broken down by race and sex.

The interaction among race, ethnicity, and sex must be examined. Research must be undertaken

to examine the ways in which students are identi-
fied as in need of special services and the content
of the special services they eventually receive.
Special-education legislation requires the develop-
ment of an individual education plan; equity in
terms of gender, race, and culture must be part of
this plan.

[1] S. A. Vogel, "Gender Differences in Intelligence, Language, Visual-Motor Abilities, and Academic Achievement in Students with Learning Disabilities: A Review of the Literature," *Journal of Learning Disabilities* 23 (January 1990):44–52.

[2] S. Shaywitz, et al., "Prevalence of Reading Disability in Boys and Girls: Results of the Connecticut Longitudinal Study," *Journal of the American Medical Association* vol. 264 (August 22/29 1990):998–1002; D. McGuinnes, "Behavioral Tempo in Pre-school Boys and Girls," *Learning and Individual Differences* 2 (1990):315–25; P. Phipps, "The LD Learner Is Often a Boy—Why?" *Academic Therapy* 17 (March 1982):425–30; C. Berry, S. Shaywitz, and B. Shaywitz, "Girls with Attention Deficit Disorder: A Silent Minority? A Report on Behavioral and Cognitive Characteristics," *Pediatrics* 76 (November 1985):801–9; A. Karlen, R. Hagin, and R. Beecher, "Are Boys Really More Vulnerable to Learning Disability than Girls?" *Academic Psychology Bulletin* 7 (Winter 1985):317–25.

[3] 1988 Elementary and Secondary School Civil Rights Survey. U.S. Department of Education, Office of Civil Rights. The survey is based on a representative sample of 4,556 public school districts and 40,020 individual schools. The Office of Civil Rights cautions that the data are for the "sample frame populations only, based on data submitted by the school districts in the sample."

compared at middle school and high school, the highest performers were boys who had been in a Montessori class where the pace and format of instruction were guided by the individual child's interests. The next highest group were girls in a more didactic program that emphasized formal group instruction. Researchers noted that "the [formal] program did contain many manipulative materials, but because of the group format these materials were not typically used for long periods of time by individuals but more often in the context of taking turns."[7] While the more formal, didactic program relied more on observation than "hands-on" experience, it also provided equal opportunities for all students to engage in some active manipulation; such opportunities are not always available for girls in coed groups, where boys tend to dominate.

The fact that one program benefited boys and the other, girls, suggests not only that many young girls may be slightly more mature and therefore able to benefit more from the group instruction offered, but also that programs that provide highly individualized instruction may unwittingly reward boys with more attention and provide girls with less precise feedback of the kind most beneficial to their learning.*

Implications

Research suggests that young girls need to be actively encouraged to participate in large-motor activities. Teachers may need to reexamine both the style with which they relate to girls and the particular content areas that are emphasized when dealing with each sex. In the preschool classroom this may mean restructuring the curriculum to include so-called "free play" activities.

The uniform application of a single preschool curriculum may not be the most effective way of improving outcomes for children. Further research is needed to

*These issues are discussed in more detail in Part Four, Chapter Two.

determine the impact of various curricula on children of different sex, race, and socioeconomic status. In the meantime, preschool programs should offer the curricular approach that most effectively serves both girls and boys or be able to modify curricula to meet the unique learning needs of each sex.

Mechanisms must be established to support teachers' attempts to modify and/or select curricula that best meet the developmental needs of both girls and boys.

ACHIEVEMENT AND PARTICIPATION: WHAT DO THE DATA SHOW?

♦

The narrowing of the gender gaps in verbal and mathematical achievement is evidence of what can be accomplished when specific attention is directed toward under-achieving groups. Remedial-reading groups and other direct attention to boys prompted by their verbal lags came first. More recently there has been increased emphasis on the importance of mathematics for girls.

There is considerable evidence that girls earn higher grades than boys throughout their school careers.[8] Test scores, however, because they measure all students on exactly the same material and are available nationally, are the measures most often used to discuss sex differences in achievement. The latest work on achievement differences presents a rather different picture from much of what has been reported and accepted in the past. The traditional wisdom that girls are better in verbal areas while boys excel in quantitative skills is less true today. Data indicate a narrowing of sex differences in tested achievement on a variety of measures.[9] However, a narrowing of differences is not an absence of differences. Important insights can be gained by looking carefully at the continuing gender gaps in educational achievement and participation. Furthermore, research that looks at sex, race, ethnicity, and socioeconomic status reveals critical vulnerabilities among various groups of girls.

Verbal Skills: Language Arts and Reading

Research does not entirely support the still-common assumption that girls do better in verbal areas than do boys. Almost twenty years ago Eleanor Maccoby and

Carol Jacklin challenged the prevailing view that girls performed better than boys on verbal measures in their early years.[10] However, researchers continued to document that girls outscored boys on tests of verbal ability starting at grade five or six.[11] Recent work indicates that sex differences in verbal abilities have decreased markedly. Researchers completing a meta-analysis comparing earlier studies of verbal abilities with more recent research conclude: "There are not gender differences in verbal ability at least at this time, in American culture, in the standard ways that verbal ability has been measured."[12]

Some researchers argue that girls do have certain verbal advantages but that these are not adequately measured by most tests.[13] Furthermore, although boys have outscored girls on the verbal section of the Scholastic Achievement Test (SAT) since 1972, some suggest this may merely reflect the inclusion of more scientifically oriented items on which boys often perform better than do girls.[14] An additional difficulty with the SAT is that test-takers are not a nationally representative sample; they are a self-selected group.

Reading

A review of three representative surveys of reading skills indicates a mixed picture. In two major surveys—the National Assessment of Educational Progress (NAEP) and the National Education Longitudinal Survey (NELS)—girls perform better than boys on reading tests. In the High School and Beyond Survey (HSB), boys perform better than girls on reading and vocabulary tests. In all three surveys, the sex differences are very small.

NAEP is the most comprehensive survey of achievement. A congressionally mandated project of the National Center for Education Statistics (NCES), it measures the proficiency of nine-year-olds, thirteen-year-olds, and seventeen-year-olds in a variety of disciplines. In all age groups, girls have consistently received higher test scores in reading and writing since the 1970s. Since 1971, however, boys have made gains relative to girls, particularly in the seventeen-year-old group.[15]

The NELS is a longitudinal survey of eighth-graders also being conducted under the auspices of NCES. The first wave of eighth-graders were interviewed and tested in 1988. Mean test scores for girls were higher than those for boys, although the difference was modest. Girls were less likely to score below "basic" and more likely to be rated as "advanced" when compared to boys.[16] This sex difference is found for all racial and ethnic groups.

The HSB, also sponsored by NCES, is a longitudinal study of high school sophomores and seniors begun in 1980. Contrary to the other studies, boys consistently score better than girls on the HSB reading tests. This is true of sophomores and seniors, and for whites, blacks, and Hispanics.[17] One possible explanation for the differences in these surveys is that sex differences narrow as children grow older. This would be consistent with the very small difference found for seventeen-year-olds in the NAEP and the gains boys make relative to girls in the follow-up of the HSB cohort.[18]

Another explanation is that these differences may reflect differences in the tests given for each survey. The HSB tests were shorter and the NAEP tests much more comprehensive. This could prove to be another case where apparent sex differences may instead reflect test differences rather than differences in the test-takers' knowledge or ability.

Even within the NAEP reading test, the performance of boys relative to girls varied, depending on the type of reading exercise. Boys did as well as girls on the expository passages and were most disadvantaged relative to girls in the literary passages. This is consistent with the finding that boys read more nonfiction than girls, and girls read more fiction than boys.[19] This is also consistent with the finding that boys do slightly better than girls on other NAEP tests in subjects requiring good skills in expository reading and writing: civics, history, and geography.[20]

If, as some suggest, boys regard fiction as more "feminine," any advantage girls experience relative to boys in the NAEP may reflect culturally defined biases against boys' reading certain kinds of material.[21] It has been suggested that even if the small gender difference favoring girls is *statistically significant*, it may not be *educationally significant*.[22] Boys still do better than girls in almost every other subject tested by NAEP, and the difference in reading scores appears to narrow and possibly even favor boys in older age groups.

Finally, it has also been argued that gender differences in reading favoring girls may be more pronounced among low-achieving or low-income students.[23] This is particularly relevant given the recent heightening of concern about the education of low-income minority boys. An examination of achievement by race, sex, and social class is presented later in this section.

Writing

Writing skills are tested less frequently. NAEP data do indicate that girls consistently outperform boys on writing-skills assessment.[24] Smaller studies of particular populations do not always support these national findings. A seven-year longitudinal study comparing the development of written language skills of boys and girls from kindergarten through grade six found that—at least in the population studied—neither sex had an advantage over the other.[25]

Mathematics and Science

The past fifteen years have seen an explosion of research on the relationship between gender and mathematics. While there has been less study on the linkage of gender and science there still is sufficient information to draw preliminary conclusions. However, the usual cautions apply. Most of the research does not break down the data by both race/ethnicity and gender. Furthermore, the interactions of race/ethnicity and gender are rarely studied, and most conclusions based on predominantly white respondents cannot be generalized to women and girls of color.[26]

ACHIEVEMENT IN MATHEMATICS. Gender differences in mathematics achievement are small and declining. Recent meta-analyses have found only very small differences in female and male performance in mathematics. Furthermore, meta-analyses comparing recent research with studies done in 1974 indicate a significant decline in gender differences.[27] The High School and Beyond study of high school sophomores and seniors also shows that gender differences favoring boys in mathematics are declining.[28]

Gender differences in mathematics do exist but are related to the age of the sample, how academically selective it is, and which cognitive level the test is tapping. Indeed these three variables were found to account for 87 percent of the variance in one meta-analysis.[29] For example, no gender differences were found in the problem-solving ability of elementary- and middle-school girls and boys, but moderate to small differences favoring males emerged in high school.[30] Large research studies support these results, finding no gender differences in math performance at age nine, minimal differences at age thirteen, and a larger difference favoring males at age seventeen.[31] The most recent National Assessment of Educational Progress (NAEP) report finds few gender-related differences in math ability in grades four and eight other than a higher average proficiency in measurement and estimation for boys. However, by grade twelve males showed a small advantage in every content area except algebra.[32]

Larger differences are found at the higher academic and cognitive levels. For example, an earlier NAEP report stated that 8.2 percent of the males but only 4.5 percent

> "**B**y the year 2000, U.S. students will be first in the world in science and mathematics achievement."[1]
>
> If the United States is to remain competitive in world markets, the nation must have a technologically competent work force. Furthermore, American democracy cannot flourish in the twenty-first century without a scientifically literate citizenry. Thus, the achievement and participation of girls—and of boys from all racial and ethnic groups—is a topic of considerable importance to policymakers in business and industry as well as education.
>
> [1] Goal Four, National Education Goals (Washington, DC: National Governors Association, 1990).

of the females were at the highest math levels, while 54 percent of the males and 48 percent of the females could do moderately complex procedures and reasoning.[33] The College Board reports that males in 1988 scored an average of 37 points higher than females on the Level I Math Achievement Test and 38 points higher on the Level II Math Achievement Test.[34] Another study revealed that nearly all differences in math performance between girls and boys at ages eleven and fifteen could be accounted for by differences among those scoring in the top 10–20 percent, with boys more often in the top-scoring groups. However, in classroom work, girls' math grades are as high as or higher than boys'.[35]

Gender differences on the SAT-Math have decreased, although they are still large. Between 1978 and 1988 female scores increased by eleven points while male scores increased by four points. However, males still outscored females 498 to 455.[36] The Educational Testing Service does test a demographically matched sample of girls and boys on the Preliminary Scholastic Aptitude Test (PSAT) each year. From 1960 through 1983 gender differences in math from this group declined, although males still slightly outscored females.[37]

A smaller body of research tying both gender and ethnicity to math achievement indicates that the patterns may differ for various groups. A study in Hawaii found non-Caucasian girls outperforming boys in math and outnumbering boys in the highest-achieving groups.[38] Other studies have reported fewer gender differences in mathematics for minority students than for white students.[39]

Gender differences in tests of spatial skills are also declining. One large study found that girls and boys gained equally from instruction in spatial-visualization skills, despite initial differences.[40]

The research results reported here must be examined in light of the achievement of all American students, female and male, in mathematics. An international assessment of the mathematics skills of thirteen-year-olds found United States students scoring below students in the other four countries and four Canadian provinces participating. Korean students had the highest average score (567.8), while the U.S. students scored 473.9.[41] In addition, the most recent National Assessment of Educational Progress reports that more than a quarter of fourth-graders failed to demonstrate the ability to do arithmetical reasoning, and only 5 percent of high school seniors demonstrated the skills needed for high technology or college-level work.[42]

ACHIEVEMENT IN SCIENCE. Gender differences in science achievement are not decreasing and may be increasing. While no meta-analyses of studies linking gender and science achievement have been done, the National Assessment of Educational Progress does track science performance. Its results indicate that for nine- and thirteen-year-olds, gender differences in achievement increased between 1978 and 1986, due to the combination of a lag in performance for females and significant increases in the performance of males. According to the NAEP, gender differences in science achievement are largest for seventeen-year-olds, and these differences have not changed since 1978. The areas of largest male advantage are physics, chemistry, earth science, and space sciences.[43]

In addition, gender differences exist at various levels of achievement. NAEP found only 5 percent of seventeen-year-old girls as compared to 10 percent of seventeen-year-old boys scoring at or above NAEP's "highest cognitive level," defined as students' ability to integrate specialized knowledge.[44] SAT achievement test scores show a similar pattern. The Educational Testing Service reports that in 1988, males scored on average 29 points higher than females on biology achievement tests. This, incidentally, was the only science area tested by ETS where gender differences declined; the spread between male and female test scores shrunk eleven points from the forty-point gap measured in 1981. Males also scored about fifty-six points higher than females on the 1988 physics achievement tests.[45] However, once again girls receive grades in science that are as high or higher than those of boys.[46]

As with gender differences in mathematics achievement, gender differences in science should be looked at in a larger context. American students, both female and male, are not doing well in science. Their low levels of scientific knowledge, even at the factual level, have been documented in both national and international studies. One international assessment of the science skills of thirteen-year-olds found United States students placing ninth among the twelve nations and provinces participating.[47]

MATHEMATICS PARTICIPATION. Gender differences in math-course participation are small, occur only in higher-level courses, and appear to be stable. In 1989 the National Science Board of the National Science Foundation reported that from 1982 to 1987, the average number of math credits that a male high school student received increased from 2.61 to 3.04. During the same time period, the average number of math credits that a female student received increased from 2.46 to 2.93. In 1982 males received .15 more math credits than females; in 1987, .11 more. The National Science Board found that approximately the same percentages of females and males took the same math courses up to calculus, which was taken by 7.6 percent of the boys but only 4.7 percent of the girls.[48] The 1991 NAEP reports that for the District of Columbia and the thirty-seven states participating in the study "Up to Algebra III/Pre-Calculus and Calculus there were no gender differences in either course-taking or average proficiency."[49] These results are similar to the findings of a 1990 survey by the Council of Chief State School Officers.[50]

SCIENCE PARTICIPATION. Gender differences in the number of science courses students take are small. However, the pattern of course-taking differs, with girls being more apt to take advanced biology and boys being more apt to take physics and advanced chemistry. In 1989 the National Science Board of the National Science Foundation reported that from 1982 to 1987, the average number of science and computer-science credits a male high school student received increased from 2.25 to 2.69. During the same time period the average number of science credits a female student received increased from 2.13 to 2.57. In both 1982 and 1987, males received .12 more science credits than did females.[51] Another study based on 1987 data reports young women taking .2 fewer science courses than young men (2.93 versus 3.13).[52] Using 1988 data, the National Science Foundation reported girls taking an average of 3.1 science courses compared to boys' 3.3.[53]

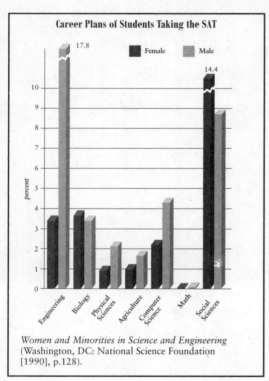

Career Plans of Students Taking the SAT

Female   Male

percent

17.8
14.4

Engineering   Biology   Physical Sciences   Agriculture   Computer Science   Math   Social Sciences

Women and Minorities in Science and Engineering (Washington, DC: National Science Foundation [1990], p.128).

All three studies found approximately the same numbers of females and males taking Biology I and Chemistry I but more males taking physics. In 1987 the National Science Board reported 25.3 percent of the males but only 15 percent of the females took physics. This is, however, an improvement. In 1982, 18.2 percent of the males but only 10 percent of the females enrolled in physics.[54]

These results are mirrored by a 1991 survey by the Council of Chief State School Officers. The survey reports that 60 percent of the students enrolled in first-year high school physics are male and that 70 percent of second-year physics students are male.[55]

CAREER PLANS. Gender differences show up in career plans as well. The bar graph on this page shows large differences between young women and men in terms of future career plans, even within the math and science fields.

High school girls, even those with exceptional academic preparation in math and science, are choosing math/science careers in disproportionately low numbers.[56] A study of Rhode Island seniors found that 64 percent of the male students who had taken physics and calculus were planning to major in science or engineering in college compared to only 18.6 percent of the female students who had taken these courses.[57]

Girls who do go on in scientific fields after high school report that the encouragement provided by their teachers is very important.[58] One study reports that girls who went on to study engineering felt that teachers encouraged them; unfortunately they also felt that counselors discouraged them.[59] Clearly, differential treatment on the basis of sex contributes to the student choices reported here, but there are other factors as well.

MATH AND SCIENCE INFLUENCES. As they grow, girls and boys have different science experiences. Girls are more apt to be exposed to biology-related activities and less apt to engage in mechanical and electrical activities.[60] One study found that by third grade, 51 percent of boys and 37 percent of girls had used microscopes, while by eleventh grade 49 percent of males and 17 percent of females had used an electricity meter.[61] Gender differences in science-related activities may be reinforced in schools if children are allowed always to select science topics based on familiarity or interest.

Eighth-grade boys have been found to use more science instruments in class, particularly physical-science tools, such as power supplies.[62] Although nine-year-old girls express interest in many science activities, they do not do as many as boys. This gender difference continues through ages thirteen and seventeen and is paralleled by an increasingly negative view of science, science classes, and science careers on the part of girls.[63]

Gender differences in confidence are strongly correlated with continuation in math and science classes. Math confidence is the surety a student has of her or his ability to learn and perform well in mathematics.[64] Math confidence has been found to be more highly correlated with math performance than any other affective variable.[65]

Females, more than males, have been found to doubt their confidence in math.[66] The Educational Testing Service reports that gender differences in perceptions of being good at math increase with age. Third-grade girls and boys think they are good in math in about the same percentages (64 percent versus 66 percent); by seventh grade, 57 percent of the girls agree, compared to 64 percent of the boys; by eleventh grade the gap widens to 48 percent of girls versus 60 percent of boys.[67] In a classic study, researchers Elizabeth Fennema and Julia Sherman found a strong correlation between math achievement and confidence. Their research revealed a drop in both girls' math confidence and their achievement in the middle-school years.[68] The drop in confidence *preceded* a decline in achievement.

One result of this diminished confidence is a lowering of the role that competence plays in girls' decisions about continuing in math and science. Researchers have found that competence is a more important prerequisite for the attainment of male career ambitions than it is for females.[69] That is, females and males often abandon math and science for different reasons. Males who drop out of math and science tend to do so because of a lack of competence—they cannot do the work; many females who drop out do so even though they can do the work.

Other researchers have also found that males are more apt than females to attribute their success to ability, while females are more apt to attribute failure to lack of ability.[70] As boys get older, those who do not like math are more likely to attribute this feeling to the

INTERVENTIONS

....

While there are few follow-up evaluations of special programs for girls in math and science, those that are available indicate that interventions can make a difference. For example, six months after attending a one-day career conference, girls' math and science career interests and course-taking plans were higher than they were prior to the conference.[1]

Three years of follow-up of an annual four-week summer program on math/science and sports for groups of "average" minority junior-high girls found the girls increased their math and science course-taking plans an average of 40 percent and are actually taking the courses.[2] Two and a half years of follow-up of a two-week residential science institute for minority and white high school juniors—all girls—already interested in science found that the program decreased the participants' stereotypes about people who were good in science, reduced their feelings of isolation, and strengthened their commitment to careers in math and science.[3] An ethnographic study of Girls Incorporated's Operation SMART found that "while girls showed some initial reluctance when

"In Eureka science we get to do experiments every day and discuss and help our peers, but in school science you can't talk among your friends about the work or you will get into trouble.. you can't experiment every day in school because you are supposed to have covered a certain amount of work by the end of the year."

Latina middle school girl

(continued from previous page)

faced with the unfamiliar [in science], with minimal encouragement and modeling, they soon set to exploring everything from snakes to environmental chemistry."[4]

Most of these programs are not a part of the official school curriculum, but they provide important avenues to explore when considering possible intervention strategies.

[1] K. Anton and S. Humphreys, *Expanding Your Horizons: 1982 Evaluation Reports* (Berkeley: Math Science Network, 1982).

[2] P. Campbell, *Eureka! Participant Follow-Up Analysis,* (Groton, MA: Campbell-Kibler Associates [1990]).

[3] P. Campbell, Douglass Science Institute: *Three Years of Encouraging Young Women in Math, Science, Engineering* (Groton, MA: Campbell-Kibler Associates, 1990).

[4] H. Nicholson and J. Frederick, *The Explorer's Pass: A Report on Case Studies of Girls and Math, Science and Technology* (New York: Girls Incorporated, 1991).

subject itself: they don't like math, they say, because it is "not useful." Girls, instead, interpret their problems with math as personal failures.[71]

Concern about the difficulty or competitiveness of the field can also be an issue. One study found that the perceived competitiveness of engineering was seen by girls as a major barrier to women entering the field.[72] This finding is supported by research that shows girls who see themselves as highly competitive to be more interested in taking math and science courses than other girls.[73] For boys, the degree of competitiveness is not related to interest in taking math and science.

While most students who dislike math do so because

they consider it too hard, most students who dislike science say science is "not interesting." Adolescent girls are more likely than adolescent boys to find science uninteresting. Adolescent boys are more likely than girls to discount the importance of science itself.[74]

In general, students' interest in and enthusiasm for math and science decline the longer they are in school. The poll commissioned by the American Association of University Women in 1990 found that enthusiasm for math and science was greatest for students in elementary school and lowest for students in high school. However, the gap between the reponses of younger and older girls was greater than the gap between younger and older boys.[75]

In addition, males are more apt than females to envision themselves using math as adults.[76] In assessing what factors they used to decide whether or not to continue math study, students listed the usefulness of math, followed by their confidence in their ability and their enjoyment of the subject.[77]

Gender stereotyping also appears to influence whether girls persist in mathematics. Data from the National Assessment of Educational Progress indicate that girls who reject traditional gender roles have higher math achievement than girls who hold more stereotyped expectations. Moreover, girls in advanced math classes tend not to see math as a "male" subject.[78]

Meta-analysis of affective variables associated with taking math courses indicates that gender differences are all small with the exception of the view of math as "something men do." Boys see math as very "male."[79] A longitudinal study that tested students at sixth,

"In our school it's 'cool' to fail and be stupid. So sometimes I've pretended that I'm not smar ."

Teenage girl quoted in "Fresh Voices," *Parade* magazine, February 10, 1991.

eighth, tenth, and twelfth grades found that for girls a view of math as "male" was negatively correlated with math achievement at each grade level. This was the only affective variable for which consistent gender differences were found.[80]

Implications

It is important that equal attention be given to both girls and boys in teaching reading and writing skills. The assumption that boys are in greater need of instruction in these areas should not be made. Furthermore, girls need particular encouragement to read more broadly in nonfiction areas and boys should be encouraged to read more fiction.

The gender gap is closing in math achievement but not in science achievement. Issues of gender and math have received more attention than issues of gender and science. Much of the work that has been done in science—beyond counting who is taking what courses—has been done in biology, a field in which there are many women, as opposed to physics, a field with very few women.

Since the growing gender gap in science is clearly related to males' climbing test scores, we need to ask why reforms in science education are apparently working for males and not for females. Just as the SAT-Math has been studied and found to underpredict women's achievement, science tests need to be checked for bias as well.

Building on the work done in math, we need to study more fully the possible causes of the gender gap in the sciences. Particular emphasis should be placed on issues of confidence.

Once students satisfy math and science requirements for graduation and college admission, gender differences in science and math course-taking emerge. More students are taking more science and math, but at the advanced levels the gender gap remains constant. It appears that messages about math and science as criti-

THERE IS NO MATH GENE

Despite the fact that the specter of a math gene favoring males is often in the news, there is strong evidence against arguments for biological/genetic causes of gender differences in math. These include:

♦ The gender gap in mathematics is rapidly decreasing; genetic differences tend to remain stable.

♦ The gap can be reduced or eliminated by changing teaching practices and providing opportunities for both girls and boys to practice building math skills; biological differences are not so easily influenced.

♦ Gender differences in math achievement are not consistent across racial/ethnic groups. If there were a sex-linked math gene, differences would be consistent across all groups.

The findings that gifted seventh-grade boys are much more likely than girls to score well on the SAT-Math, often used to suggest a biological basis for math gender differences, are seriously flawed because the researchers

♦ assume that because girls and boys have been in the same math classes, they have had the same experiences;

(continued from previous page)

♦ *do not look at effects of differential treatment in and out of the classroom;*

♦ *use the SAT in part because it finds larger gender differences than other standardized tests;*

♦ *postulate a biological basis for differences in SAT scores, whereas ETS has reported that this test underpredicts girls' performance and overpredicts boys';*

♦ *assume that gifted children whose parents pay more than $30 for their children to take a test represent the population as a whole;*

♦ *indicate in written materials sent to students before they take the SAT that girls do not do as well as boys.[1]*

[1] P. Campbell, T. Kibler and K. Campbell-Kibler, "Taking the SAT at Twelve: One Family's View of Talent Search," *College Prep* (7) (1991): 8–10.

cal assets for later employment have been somewhat successful, at least for middle-school students. However, while we have more girls taking more math and science, the numbers and percentages of girls interested in careers in math and science is increasing minimally, if at all. During senior high school and college, female students drop out of the math/science pipeline because they choose not to pursue scientific careers.[81]

Changing the public images of physics and chemistry to reflect the diversity of these fields and the way they tie in to our everyday lives can provide more girls with the "inside information" that daughters of scientists appear to get. Meeting, getting to know, and working with scientists also reduces negative and intimidating stereotypes about the field. Providing students, especially girls, with more real-life experiences with science and scientists may make a big difference.

Teaching methods to decrease or eliminate the gender gaps in math and science already exist. Having students read and try out math and science problems before they are covered in class appears to narrow the "experience" gap between girls and boys, thus helping to reduce gender differences in class performance.[82] Providing a structure in which all students answer questions, pose questions, and receive answers, rather than one that emphasizes target students or those who call out answers loudest, increases girls' opportunities and interest. Girls also respond well to special programs where they work cooperatively in a relaxed atmosphere where math is fun. Such programs significantly increase the number of math and science courses girls take. However, while hands-on experience is more successful than the lecture approach, such experiences must allow sufficient time and opportunities for girls to reach the same level of performance that teachers expect from boys.[83]

Schools can learn much from out-of-school programs that encourage girls in math and science. Girls are not required to take special out-of-school programs. Designers of successful out-of-school math and science programs have learned how to get girls to attend and, more important, how to keep them interested so that they will keep on attending. We need to continue and expand programs like those developed by Girls, Incorporated; the Girl Scouts; and several AAUW branches. These offer unique opportunities for girls to learn together to overcome stereotypes. What's more, such programs also act as laboratories for developing effective techniques to keep girls involved in math and science. We can't rely on these programs alone, however. Compared to the school system, they can reach only small numbers of girls for relatively short periods of time. Since all girls go to school and go for many years, we must focus most of our effort there, incorporating techniques that work for girls throughout our schools, and doing so in ways that continue to work for girls systemwide.

RACE, SEX, SOCIOECONOMIC STATUS, AND ACADEMIC ACHIEVEMENT

♦

As noted in the discussion on reading achievement, some research indicates that sex-based performance differences favoring girls may be more pronounced among low-income students. This suggests that sex differences can cut either way, depending on social class. It follows that gender studies can help us understand the educational needs of boys as well as girls.

Unfortunately, little recent data have been published that permit an examination of student achievement by sex, race or ethnicity, and socioeconomic status (SES). In addition, little information is available on sex differences and gender issues in key programs funded by the U.S. Department of Education. A literature search produced almost no recent information on differences among girls and boys in compensatory (remedial), American Indian, or bilingual education programs.[84] This is particularly disheartening, considering that these programs constitute more than 20 percent of the Department of Education budget—compensatory education alone represents two-thirds of the budget of the Office of Elementary and Secondary Education. These programs play a crucial role in meeting the educational needs of low-income and minority students, although at current funding levels, less than half of those eligible receive these services.[85]

"**F**ew research studies have focused on both race and gender; moreover, researchers have frequently confounded socioeconomic status with minority group membership."

D. Scott-Jones and M. Clark, "The School Experiences of Black Girls: The Interaction of Gender, Race and Socioeconomic Status," *Phi Delta Kappan*, vol. 67 #7, 1986, p. 520.

A special analysis was conducted using data from the National Educational Longitudinal Survey (NELS) of eighth-graders for 1988 and High School and Beyond (HSB) for 1980. These data compare grades, test scores in reading and mathematics, and post-school plans in terms of students' sex, race or ethnicity, and socioeconomic status. Data were examined for blacks, whites, American Indians, Asians, and Hispanics. These groups were further broken down by sex and socioeconomic status (ranked either "high-SES" or "low-SES").[86] Some sample sizes were too small to report, particularly in the case of Asians and American Indians. The results are summarized below.[87]

Socioeconomic status is the best predictor of both grades and test scores, but there are important sex and racial/ethnic differences. As expected, girls get better grades than boys in both data sets, even when controlling for socioeconomic status. One exception is high-SES black girls, whose grades are similar to rather than better than their male counterparts in the HSB data. Asian girls consistently outperform all other race/sex groups.

While student performance and career plans often vary by race, many of the differences narrow dramatically when students from the same socioeconomic group are compared. Among eighth-graders, low-SES whites are more likely than similar blacks and Hispanics to have poor marks, although this difference is not found in the high school data. The data confirm what has been known for many years: that socioeconomic status, more than any other variable, predicts educational outcomes.[88]

The limits that socioeconomic status set on achievement are most obvious from observing test scores in reading and mathematics. The data are most dramatic in the eighth-grade sample. Very few low-SES students score in the advanced reading or in the advanced math category; very few high-SES students fall below the basic skills level in reading or math. This is true regardless of race or gender. Contrary to popular myth, low-SES Asian students do not fare significantly better than other low-SES students in their eighth-grade test scores.

Among low-SES eighth-graders, girls are less likely than boys to test below basic levels in reading and math. At higher SES levels, however, girls lose this edge. Among high-SES eighth-graders, girls are no more likely than boys to be in advanced reading, and they are less likely to be in advanced math. Thus there is a marked bipolarity in the relative achievement of eighth-grade girls: those of low socioeconomic status are more likely to do better than similar boys, while those at high socioeconomic status are only as likely and often less likely to do as well as boys.

These findings raise provocative questions. Are more resources devoted to high-SES boys relative to high-SES girls than are provided to low-SES boys relative to low-SES girls? Do boys of low socioeconomic status invest less in their education because they see their future job prospects as more limited than girls'? Does low socioeconomic status have a differential effect on the development of boys? In light of the current policy attention to the particular education problems of poor black and Hispanic boys, it is interesting to note that among most low-SES students, most boys do less well than girls, regardless of race, and that these differences in academic performance do not persist at higher socioeconomic levels, at least in terms of test scores.[89] This suggests that closer attention should be paid to the combined impact of gender and social class, as well as race, on education outcomes.

Among low-SES high school students, girls test no better than boys. This change from the eighth-grade pattern possibly reflects higher dropout rates among boys of low socioeconomic status together with real gains made by those boys who stay in school. The HSB data do not show any sex differences favoring girls in high school test scores, even among less-privileged students. In the senior year follow-up of the sophomore sample, sex differences generally favor males. This does not discount the findings in NELS. The eighth-graders are a later group, tested in 1988; high school sophomores in the HSB sample were tested in 1980, two years after they were eighth-graders themselves. Thus there is a full ten years' difference in the samples. More important, an analysis shows that some low-SES males dropped out before the HSB sample was drawn; the greater similarity in scores between girls and boys may simply reflect fewer low-performing boys in the sample.[90] Nevertheless, the data show that those boys who do stay in school make real gains in test scores relative to girls as they approach graduation.

Among high-SES students, boys clearly do better than girls in high school. The differences are most striking among black students: boys are well ahead of girls in reading and math scores. Male dropouts have not skewed the results here. Dropping out is minimal among students of high socioeconomic status. Something else is responsible—perhaps the school environment in which these black students are learning. Research on black students in desegregated schools indicates that black girls do not do as well as boys in this environment, often feeling excluded and socially isolated. Thus the fact that high-SES black youngsters are more likely to be in desegregated schools may explain the relatively poorer performance of high-SES black girls.[91]

The NELS data also show that among low-SES students, boys are more likely than girls to have repeated at least one grade. This holds almost equally true for black, white, and Hispanic boys. Black girls are more like their male counterparts in this respect than girls in any other group.

An extraordinary one-third of all low-SES boys are held back at least one grade. In spite of the media attention placed specifically on black boys, 29 percent of low-SES black girls also were held back at least one grade.

Percentage of Eighth-graders Who Have Repeated at Least One Grade (broken down by race, sex, and socioeconomic status)	Low-SES		High-SES	
	Females	Males	Females	Males
American Indian	27	41	3	17
Asian	15	26	5	5
Black	29	34	7	10
Hispanic	23	34	9	13
White	24	33	5	10

Source: Unpublished data from the NELS.

Even after adjusting for SES, racial and ethnic differences persist in both data sets. Grading differences, by race, among low-SES students tend to be small, but high-SES whites and Asians do better than their counterparts. Similarly, comparing students from the same SES groups diminishes some but not all racial differences in test scores. Asians and whites generally earn higher test scores than blacks and Hispanics.

There are several possible explanations. First, racial and ethnic minorities are more likely to attend poor schools with fewer resources. The persistence of racial segregation in housing means that non-poor blacks are more likely to live in poor neighborhoods (and therefore attend schools in low-income neighborhoods) than are similar whites.[92] Thus SES is not a perfect arbiter of access to good schools. Second, teachers' expectations of and interactions with minority girls and boys affect outcomes. These patterns are discussed in greater detail later in this report. Third, according to researcher John Ogbu, children who feel that they will be consigned to low-caste jobs because of their race or caste status have little motivation to excel in school.[93] Educational achievement must be examined within the overall social-cultural context and its influences on children's expectations about school and work.

The HSB data show that even though boys have similar or better test scores than girls, girls are more likely to express an interest in college. This is particularly true among high-SES students. Male seniors overall express a greater interest in work or the military right after school. Black males in particular, and Hispanic males to a lesser extent, express a much greater interest in the military than do whites, even when controlling for SES or test scores.

These sex-based differences in college plans are exemplified by data on students taking advanced-placement (AP) exams.[94] Among those taking AP exams in 1990, 52 percent were girls. Morever, black and Hispanic girls are more likely to take AP exams than are boys from the same groups: among black test takers, 64 percent were girls; among Hispanic test takers, 56 to 60 percent were girls.[95]

Gender differences persist in the types of exams taken. Girls are less likely to take exams in math and science. Nevertheless, since so many more black girls than boys are taking AP exams, they outnumber black boys in all advanced-placement fields except art and music. This is not true for any other group. Hispanic girls, for example, outnumber boys in total tests taken but take fewer math and science exams than Hispanic boys.

The AP data do not reflect differences in assignments to AP courses. In the HSB data, boys are as likely as girls—regardless of race or ethnicity—to be placed in AP courses in high school.

Further, socioeconomic status alone does not explain girls' greater interest in college. Most students taking AP exams are high-SES students. Low-SES students generally do not do well enough in school, regardless of race or ethnicity, to be in AP classes, and the AP exam is not available in all schools. Rather, these results may reflect the perception by some boys that they can do just as well working (which, to some extent, is true for white males) and the perception by others (particularly black males) that the military may be a more desirable alternative to college.

Implications

While of great interest, these results from the NELS and HSB data are merely suggestive; more detailed and sophisticated research is needed. One limitation is the small sample sizes for some groups, particularly Asians and American Indians. Recent demographic changes resulting in a more diverse school population require greater attention to the inclusion of all students in the design of surveys and in the study of student achievement. There must also be greater sensitivity to within-group diversity in terms of sex and SES. It is clear from this research and that of others, however, that since black, Hispanic, and American Indian students are more likely to be poor, they suffer disproportionately. Public schools must do more to provide educational opportunity for children of low socioeconomic status, who do less well in school regardless of race/ethnicity or sex. As Jonathan Kozol eloquently points out in his recent book, *Savage Inequalities*, there is something terribly wrong with the way we finance education in this country.[96] Educational excellence and equity can never be achieved until we devote substantial financial resources to poor children.[97]

TEEN PREGNANCY AND MOTHERHOOD

♦

Teen pregnancy and teen motherhood have been the focus of considerable public-policy concern for more than two decades. Some experts now challenge assumptions that the threat associated with early childbearing is as great as research has indicated.[98] In the view of these experts, the focus on teenage pregnancy and childbearing draws public attention away from deeper structural sources of family stress. In fact, early childbearing may be an adaptive response to social and economic deprivation. Many teenage girls are deeply disadvantaged before they have children, and like others from disadvantaged backgrounds they face long odds of doing well later in life whether or not they become pregnant at an early age.[99] It is an important perspective to keep in mind when examining data on early pregnancy and motherhood.

"**Pregnancy** is only one of the things our students have to deal with. Most have been victims all their lives—victims of poverty, of physical, sexual, and emotional abuse."

Dorotha Hogue, AAUW Educational Foundation Eleanor Roosevelt Teacher Fellowship recipient, Florence Crittenden School, Denver, Colorado.

Incidence of Births to Adolescents

In 1988, just under one-half million babies were born to women under age twenty in the United States, giving this country the highest rate of teenage childbearing in the Western industrialized world.[100] Overall, the number and rate of births to teens continues a downward trend begun in 1975.[101] However, among fifteen- to seventeen-year-olds there is a 10 percent increase in births, almost entirely among black and Hispanic teens.[102] Data from the National Survey of Family Growth suggest that one explanation for this increase is that the number of fifteen-year-olds with sexual experience increased from 17 percent in 1980 to 26 percent in 1988.[103]

Costs

The public cost of families formed by teens is high. In 1989, the United States spent nearly $21.5 billion on Aid to Families with Dependent Children (AFDC), Medicaid, and food-stamp benefits for families begun by teenage mothers.[104] This amount was $1.7 billion higher than for 1988. Though inflation played a role, the figures also reflect an increase in births to teens, especially among fifteen- to seventeen-year-olds.[105] Fifty-nine percent of women who received AFDC payments in 1988 were nineteen or younger at the birth of their first child.[106] Among children age five or younger who were living in poverty in 1988, nearly half lived in families begun by teen mothers.[107]

Keeping pregnant teenagers and young mothers in school and helping them gain the skills they need to support themselves and their children received explicit recognition in the 1988 Family Support Act. The Act targets teen custodial parents on AFDC and requires teens without a high school degree or its equivalent to participate in full-time educational activities leading to a diploma.

Antecedents of Adolescent Pregnancy

Sexism and sex-role stereotyping are pervasive in our society. They affect every facet of young girls' lives and play a crucial, if unacknowledged, role in creating the teen mother. Western culture has honored the role of mother above all others for women. Thus, for some adolescents, motherhood is the ultimate gender role and "an honorable escape from a race they cannot win."[1]

Several studies suggest that adolescent girls who become pregnant are more likely than their sexually active peers to be traditional in sex-role orientation. Traditional views of sex roles are also strongly correlated with lower socioeconomic status.[2] Studies that look at the differences between pregnant teens and those using or seeking birth control find that girls in the latter group are less likely to hold traditional gender-based views of self and are more likely to exhibit a sense of self-determination.[3]

Low self-esteem is also linked in some studies to increased likelihood of early pregnancy, and in some instances this low self-esteem is caused by sexual abuse.[4] The incidence of sexual victimization among teen mothers is high and may contribute to premature parenthood. In 1987 the Illinois Ounce of Prevention Fund survey found that 61 percent of a group of pregnant teens and teen mothers reported having experienced an unwanted sexual encounter. The mean age at first occurrence was 11.5.[5]

A teen's awareness of how early motherhood could jeopardize her future is a critical factor in inhibiting early childbearing.[6] This finding is confirmed in High School and Beyond (HSB) survey data that show the lowest teen motherhood rates among girls with high academic ability and upper-

(continued from previous page)

income intact families, girls with the "brightest prospects."[7]

For teens at greater risk of adolescent pregnancy, the willingness to consider having a child outside of marriage is a good predictor of outcomes two years later. Other factors linked to early pregnancy and childbearing include low academic standing, "problem behaviors" such as drug and alcohol abuse, disciplinary problems in school, absenteeism, and poor parent-child communication, but the strength of these factors varies significantly across racial and ethnic groups.[8]

The agenda for pregnancy prevention has substantially broadened with recent efforts to strengthen teenagers' motivation, as well as their capacity, to avoid pregnancy.[9] This new emphasis shifts the focus for prevention to the schools' ability to provide enrichment, social supports, health services, job preparation, and other programs designed to help disadvantaged youth.

"Fifty-two percent of all births to women under age twenty in 1980 were to married women; by 1988, this figure had dropped to 34 percent."

U.S. Department of Health and Human Services, National Center for Health Statistics, *Vital Statistics of the United States*, vol. 2, tables 1-1, 1-31, 1-81.

[1] T. Cusick, "Sexism and Early Parenting: Cause and Effect?" *Peabody Journal of Education: Issues on Sex Equity and Sexuality in Education* 64 (Fall 1987):113–31.

[2] C. Ireson, "Adolescent Pregnancy and Sex Roles," *Sex Roles* 11 (1984), pp. 189–201.

[3] S. Jorgensen and S. Alexander, "Research on Adolescent Pregnancy Risk: Implications for Sex Education Programs," *Theory into Practice* (Ohio State University) 22 (1983):125–33; S. Philpps-Yonas, "Teenage Pregnancy and Motherhood: A Review of the Literature," *American Journal of Orthopsychiatry* 50 (1980):403–31; R. Blum and M. Resnick, "Adolescent Sexual Decision-making: Contraception, Pregnancy, Abortion and Motherhood," *Pediatric Annals* 11 (1982):797–805.

[4] M. Patton, "Self Concept and Self Esteem: Factors in Adolescent Pregnancy," *Adolescence* 16 (1981):765–78; M. Press, "Sex and Sex Roles: What Are We Really Telling Kids?" *Equal Play* 7 (1988):9–10.

[5] H. Gershenon, "Taking the Romance out of Teen Pregnancy," *TEC Network*, No. 17 (Southwest Regional Laboratory, Los Alamitos, CA) (April 1988), p. 1.

[6] A. Abrahamse, P. Morrison, and L. Waite, "Beyond Stereotypes: Who Becomes a Single Teenage Mother?" (Santa Monica CA: Rand Corporation, January 1988); A. Abrahamse, P. Morrison, and L. Waite, "Teenagers Willing to Consider Single Parenthood: Who Is at Greatest Risk?" *Family Planning Perspectives* 20 (January/February 1988):13–18.

[7] Abrahamse, Morrison, and Waite, "Beyond Stereotypes."

[8] Ibid.

[9] J. Dryfoos, "Schools Get in the Act: Pregnancy Prevention Programs and Public Education," *Equal Play* 7 (1988):2–6.

School Response

Most schools halted blatant discrimination toward pregnant teens and teen mothers following the passage of Title IX of the Education Amendments of 1972. Considerable evidence still exists, however, that many schools avoid making special efforts to retain pregnant teens and teen mothers, and continue to limit the opportunities available to them.[108] A recent survey of state educational equity practices reports that several states repeatedly tried to bar pregnant students from the honor society; at least one state automatically exempts pregnant students and parents, married and unmarried, from compulsory attendance requirements.[109]

Many teachers and administrators consider these teens second-class students and often judge pregnant teens and teen mothers more harshly than they do teen fathers.[110]

Traditionally, teen pregnancy has been viewed as a female issue. Relatively little attention has been paid to the role of teen fathers in caring for and supporting their children or to the impact of fatherhood on teenage boys. Young fathers are less likely to receive a high school diploma than boys of the same age who have not fathered a child.[111] While the consequences of early childbearing are more severe for girls, the effect on boys is important to consider as well. The impact depends, in part, on the degree of responsibility fathers assume for the care and support of their children.[112] Contrary to the prevailing assumption that teen fathers are uninterested in or uninvolved with the teen mother and child, studies reveal that there is considerable diversity here.[113]

Recent attention has focused on how best to ensure that teen fathers not only assume financial responsibility for their offspring but also receive academic education, job training, and life-skills education to encourage their self-sufficiency and enhance their involvement with their children.[114] From a gender-equity perspective, since young mothers usually have greater responsibility for their children than fathers, programs that help young fathers assume

School-based clinics offer one example of a successful prevention program that provides equitable access to needed services for both girls and boys. These clinics, now in fifty schools across the country, help to ensure an integrated approach to health care, including reproductive health care. A recent evaluation of twenty-three school-based clinics, funded by the Robert Wood Johnson Foundation, found that while student enrollment was equally divided between the sexes, girls accounted for nearly two-thirds of the visits.

R. Johnson, *Access* (Washington, DC: School-Based Adolescent Health Care Program, Children's National Medical Center, Winter 1990).

more responsibility for child care and support but do not necessarily encourage marriage are viewed increasingly as in the best interests of teen mothers and their children.[115]

Effects of Teen Parent Programs

Although the research remains spotty, several recent studies suggest that community programs that offer teen parents comprehensive medical, social, and educational services for up to three years after the birth of a child have a greater impact on educational attainment, acquisition of vocational skills, delay of subsequent births, and economic self-sufficiency than do short-term programs.[116]

Schools, although often reluctant to provide services to pregnant teens and teen parents, continue to be the most important and likely places for the coordination of these services and the development of new programs. Recent studies indicate that schools are increasingly involved in providing child care programs on or near school grounds to enable teens to remain in school.[117] Case managers in the high schools are effective in providing and coordinating an array of services to pregnant students and students with children.[118] One study showed that 80 percent of the girls enrolled in such programs stayed in school.[119]

Efforts to improve options for teen parents and their children range from national demonstration models to state and local programs. In one state program, the Illinois Ounce of Prevention/Parents Too Soon Project, teen mothers who participated for twelve months had nearly one-third fewer subsequent pregnancies, were almost four times as likely to be enrolled in school, and somewhat more likely to be employed than a comparable sample.[120]

In Albuquerque, New Mexico, the New Futures School, which provides educational, vocational, health, and social services, including on-site child care for teens and teen parents, also reports encouraging results. Over a six-year period, 82 percent of all New Futures participants graduated from high school or obtained an equivalency degree, and 32 percent of this group went on to post-secondary education or training. These figures are particularly impressive given that 36 percent of the New Futures students were previous school dropouts.[121] The program's provision of on-site services is also credited with keeping participants' pregnancy rate to one-third the national average.[122]

In San Francisco, an interagency citywide comprehensive case-management service network is coordinated by the San Francisco Unified School District and a local nonprofit agency. Cross-program data on teen mothers and fathers who were tracked for six months after childbirth indicates that program participation helped these teens maintain a 60 percent school enrollment rate, three times the typical school continuation rate for young parents.[123]

> "**O**nly 54 percent of young mothers aged eighteen and nineteen—the traditional age for high school completion—had completed high school education in 1988, compared to 86 percent of older mothers. Young black mothers were slightly more likely to have completed their secondary education (57 percent) than white mothers (52 percent)."
>
> Centers for Disease Control, "Premarital Sexual Experience Among Adolescent Women: United States, 1970–1988," *Morbidity and Mortality Weekly* Report 39 (1991):929–32.

While projects like these are beginning to document their success in improving outcomes for teen mothers and their children, they are relatively few in number, and good research data is still scarce. Schools play a vital role both in equitably educating teen mothers and fathers and in ensuring their access to the range of services these students need to complete their education.

VOCATIONAL EDUCATION

◆

An analysis of the distribution of girls and women in different vocational courses of study indicates only small changes in sex-segregated patterns in recent years despite an emphasis on sex equity in federal legislation.

J. Wirt,
L. Murasicin,
D. Goodwin,
and R. Meyer,
National Assessment of Vocational Education: Summary of Findings and Recommendations (Washington, DC: U.S. Department of Education, 1989).

Vocational education was originally designed to give work skills to high school boys who were not planning to attend college. But research indicates that it may not serve either males or females very well in the current environment.[124] Although vocational courses were eventually expanded to serve girls and women, their focus tended to be on home economics. As labor market opportunities for women expanded, vocational courses were added in health and office occupations. Many educators believe that the vocational system has failed both men and women: men, because the training has had little impact on their earnings, and women, because they have been routed into sex-stereotyped course work that leads to dead-end, low-paying jobs.

Studies of the impact of secondary vocational-education training have found little or no effect on male wages, although research indicates that boys trained in high school are more likely to work longer hours (and, therefore, earn more on an annual basis) and report greater job satisfaction.[125] For girls and women, these same studies do find significant effects of vocational training in terms of wages and hours worked, but virtually all of these gains are found in sex-stereotyped jobs, particularly those in office and business occupations.[126]

The positive effect is stronger for whites than for minorities.

Studies also indicate that minorities are less likely to enroll in vocational education, even when controlling for socioeconomic status, suggesting that they may have lower expectations from vocational training than similar whites.[127] In assessing all of these studies, however, it is important to remember that the follow-up periods used are relatively short. Most examine program effects two to eight years after high school graduation. It is entirely possible that effects of training may be greater or lesser as time goes on. The latter is particularly likely for women and for minority men, who are more often in occupations with few opportunities for advancement.

The problem in part is in the labor market. Recent years have seen a tremendous expansion of job opportunities in traditionally female office and clerical occupations and a commensurate decline in traditionally male job opportunities in the trades and industries that are historically male.

It is also clear that women encounter discrimination when they enter nontraditional fields. Women trained in traditionally male jobs are less likely to be employed and more likely to earn lower wages than men receiving the same training.[128]

It is not surprising that the vocational system has been unsuccessful in moving girls and women into nontraditional jobs. According to the findings of the National Assessment of Vocational Education (NAVE), relatively few resources have been devoted to sex-equity programs.[129] Despite specific legislation focusing on sex-equity goals, sex-equity grants have been small and these have been distributed to a limited number of districts. Furthermore, researchers report significant cynicism among administrators about efforts to achieve sex equity.

Similarly, funding for single parents and displaced homemakers has gone to only a limited number of districts and not necessarily those where the need was greatest. The awards have been very small (median award: about $8,000) and most often earmarked for counseling or ancillary services. This corresponds to NAVE's findings on other special groups targeted by federal legislation. Here, too, grants have tended to be small and have been used primarily to provide services rather than to upgrade institutions in low-income areas. In addition, the study found that students in the most disadvantaged schools are 40 percent less likely than students in top schools to have access to an area vocational school. Furthermore, schools with the largest concentrations of disadvantaged students have access to 40 percent fewer vocational courses than students in the most advantaged schools.[130]

There are few role models in vocational education for women or men of color outside a narrow range of occupational fields. Within secondary schools, women teachers in vocational courses are concentrated in predictable areas. For example, women teach 98 percent of consumer and homemaking classes, 92 percent of occupational home economics classes, 90 percent of health classes, and 69 percent of office occupations classes. Women teachers are comparatively scarce in fields such as industrial arts (where they make up only 4 percent of teachers), agriculture (where they make up 6 percent), trade and industry (where they comprise 9 percent), and technical occupations (where they make up 12 percent). Minority teachers are concentrated in occupational home economics (where they represent 15 percent of all teachers), office occupations, consumer and homemaking, and industrial arts (in each of which they represent 12 percent).[131] No data are available by race and sex, but the only male-dominated field in which people of color can be found in significant numbers is industrial arts.

Since studies of vocational education indicate little success in increasing the earnings of men and in changing the occupational distribution of women, many argue that specific training should no longer be the goal of vocational education. Reformers suggest that vocational education should teach vocational students the same concepts that academically oriented students learn, except in a different setting. Conceptual and critical thinking, creativity, and other mental skills should be taught in vocational programs as a complement rather than as an alternative to academic training.

A broad range of students already participate in vocational courses on the secondary level, including students pursuing academic programs. In 1982 college-bound high school graduates had taken an average of 2.04 credits in vocational education in grades eleven and twelve, compared to their non-college-bound peers, who had taken an average of 3.77 vocational credits.[132] Thus, it is no longer appropriate to regard vocational training as a program exclusively for nonacademically oriented students. While those concentrating in a vocational program are less likely to attend college, students clearly are not viewing vocational courses as antithetical to more academic goals. In fact, college-bound students were able to increase their math proficiency by taking vocational courses offering applied mathematics.[133]

One study found that 65 percent of female high school students in nontraditional courses reported harassment by male classmates and by some teachers.

R. Kane and P. Frazee, *Women in Nontraditional Vocational Education in Secondary Schools* (Arlington, VA: RJ Associates, 1978), as reported in L.Vetter, "The Vocational Option for Women," in S. Harlan and R. Steinberg, eds., *Job Training for Women: The Promise and Limits of Public Policies* (Philadelphia, PA: Temple University Press, 1989), p. 105.

The New Law

The 1990 amendments to the Carl C. Perkins Vocational Education Act of 1984 attempt a major restructuring of vocational education. The new law lists two goals for the use of federal funds: (1) to integrate vocational and academic training, using vocational training to enhance academic skills and (2) to provide special groups—the economically disadvantaged, students with disabilities, students with limited English, and females in nontraditional programs—with services needed to ensure their full participation in vocational education.

It is unclear how the new legislation will affect girls in secondary education. The new funding formula may give girls in disadvantaged areas access to more adequately funded programs. Since low-income and minority women have the most restricted labor-market opportunities, the new legislation may improve their opportunities for training and education.

An important area of concern remains the distribution of young women among sex-stereotyped occupational fields. A policy change emphasizing the enhancement of academic skills and de-emphasizing specific occupational training may provide these young women with the skills needed to obtain higher-paying jobs. But unless we encourage girls and young women to take nontraditional courses and help place them in jobs or post-secondary institutions requiring the skills learned, any training they receive will have little effect on their labor-market opportunities.

EXTRACURRICULAR ACTIVITIES AND SPORTS

Grades, test scores, and course-taking patterns are all important aspects of students' educational experiences. But information on disparate patterns of participation in extracurricular activities among girls and boys is also revealing in terms of the status of girls in public education.

Since the 1972 passage of Title IX, which mandates equal educational opportunities in academic and athletic programs for girls and boys, girls' participation in athletics has increased dramatically. In 1972 approximately 4 percent of the female school population participated in secondary-school athletics; by 1987 the figure had risen to 26 percent.[1]

However, boys' participation is still almost twice that of girls.[2] These findings are corroborated by data from the National Educational Longitudinal Survey (NELS) of eighth-graders, which reveal that in all racial groups boys are much more likely than girls to participate in school sports. In addition, the percentage of women coaches has decreased, not increased, since the passage of Title IX. As in other areas of educational leadership, students lack female role models in athletics.[3]

A recent statewide study in Michigan revealed that students perceive clear sex-biased standards and expectations favoring males in physical education classes. Moreover, students listed almost all sports as male domains; figure skating, gymnastics, jumping rope, and cheerleading were the only athletic activities identified as female. When asked,

(continued from previous page)

"How would your life be different if you were a boy?" many girls wrote about how they would play and enjoy sports more if they were male. Obviously, gender socialization has a profound effect on how girls perceive themselves in relation to sports. Classroom teaching practices and systematic limitations in school districts play a critical role. Seventy percent of the school districts polled in this study did not provide girls with athletic opportunities comparable to those available to boys.[4]

But girls enjoy and benefit from participation in sports as much as boys do. For example, research indicates that even though the participation of Hispanic girls in high school athletics is low, they more than any other minority subgroup "were most likely to reap benefits from participating in high school athletics...[and] more apt than non-athletes to improve their academic standing while in high school, to graduate, and to attend college following high school."[5]

The NELS eighth-grade data reveal that participation in all types of extracurricular activities is consistently lower among Hispanic girls than among other girls. Asian and black girls show lower participation than white girls in most activities except science fairs and student newspaper and yearbook work, where their participation rates are as high as or higher than those of white girls.[6]

Extracurricular activities and sports provide important opportunities for leadership, teamwork, and the development of citizenship.[7] They also provide both a chance to explore a variety of new areas and an opportunity to delve into an area of particular interest if a student is so inclined.

Extracurricular activities also offer opportunities for personal contacts with adult role models who can, in turn, provide guidance and support. For all of these reasons, it is important to actively encourage girls' participation.

[1] M. Messner and D. Sabo, "Toward a Critical Feminist Reappraisal of Sport, Men and the Gender Order," in *Sport, Men and the Gender Order* (Champaign, IL: Human Kinetics Books, 1990), p. 73.

[2] *1990–1991 Handbook* (Kansas City: National Federation of State High School Associations, 1990), p. 73.

[3] T. Isaac and S. Shafer, *Sex Equity in Sports Leadership: Implementing the Game Plan in Your Community* (Lexington, KY: Eastern Kentucky University, 1989).

[4] Michigan Department of Education, Office of Sex Equity in Education, "The Influence of Gender Role Socialization on Student Perceptions," June 1990.

[5] *The Women's Sports Foundation Report, Minorities in Sports: The Effect of Varsity Sports Participation on the Social, Educational, and Career Mobility of Minority Students* (New York: Women's Sports Foundation, 1989), p. 14.

[6] Unpublished analysis of NELS data. L. Burbridge, September 1991.

[7] M. Murtaugh, "Achievement Outside the Classroom: The Role of Nonacademic Activities in the Lives of High School Students," *Anthropology and Education Quarterly* 19 (1988), pp. 383–395.

DROPPING OUT OF SCHOOL

♦

The dropout rate has become a key indicator of success for schools. But reliable, comparable data on dropouts are not readily available. In fact, there is no standard definition of a school dropout, and a variety of measures are used to calculate dropout rates. There are two sources for dropout data: the data collected by state and local education agencies and the information that can be obtained from large national surveys. Poor record keeping mars the data collected by state and local agencies. Often, students who merely transfer to other schools are recorded as dropouts, and students who return to school or to general education degree (GED) programs—after dropping out for a short period—continue to be counted as dropouts. As a result, the high school dropout rates recorded by many cities may be overstated.[134]

Dropout statistics can also be derived from national surveys such as the Current Population Survey or from

> "They don't really see your personal life, they just figure, well she is doing okay, she is doing okay. Just like they say about the kids that commit suicide. 'Well, I thought she was fine, I thought there was nothing wrong.' You know, I didn't even know my counselor 'til I dropped out of school. I didn't even know there was a counselor in school. They don't care about the one that is sitting there, not turning in work on time, they should actually."
>
> Seventeen-year-old female high school dropout, Anchorage, Alaska, as quoted in *Young Women of Alaska Speak Out About Dropping Out*, The Alaska Women's Commission, February 1990.

education surveys such as High School and Beyond, sponsored by the Department of Education. These sources are sometimes criticized because they may under-count those most at risk of dropping out—such as young minority males—and because they often do not permit detailed statistics on dropouts in specific locations. There are also disparities between what parents report for their children and what children report themselves. Further, as with state and local data, national surveys may not iden-tify dropouts who later return to school.

One detailed study examining trends in dropout rates, using data from Current Population Surveys between 1968 and 1984, focuses on those thirty-four years old or younger (thus including students who may have returned to school in their twenties and early thir-ties). This study found that since 1968, high school dropout rates for black males and females declined 40 percent, compared to a 32 percent decline for white females and a 27 percent decline for white males.[135] Overall, Hispanic dropout rates have not declined as dramatically; among eighteen- to nineteen-year-olds, however, dropout rates declined 30 to 34 percent between 1978 and 1984.

As discussed earlier in the analysis of High School and Beyond data, girls are more likely to complete high school and go on to college than are boys, regardless of race or ethnicity. Black boys and girls show dramati-cally different school-completion patterns: black girls have significantly lower dropout rates and higher col-lege enrollment rates than black boys.[136] This is not true for Hispanics, and gender differences in these areas are not as great for whites. Among Hispanics, however, school-completion patterns vary considerably by national origin: Puerto Rican and Cuban American girls are more likely to drop out of school than boys of the same cultures or than Mexican American and other Hispanic girls.[137]

Even when girls appear to be doing as well as, or better than, boys, many girls lose this advantage over time. While boys are often more likely than girls to drop out, studies show that black and Hispanic males are more likely to return to school within two years to obtain a GED than black and Hispanic females.[138] This may explain why differences in high school achievement for black males and females appear to narrow among older black men and women.

Finally, it should be noted that female dropouts have much higher poverty rates than male dropouts. Among blacks the figures are 47 percent for female dropouts compared to 29 percent for male dropouts. Among Hispanic high school dropouts, 35 percent of the females live in poverty compared to 24 percent of the males. Among whites, 23 percent of female dropouts live in poverty, compared to only 15 percent of the males.[139] Comparable figures for American Indians and Asian Americans are not available. It should be noted, however, that the economic status of Asian Americans is highly bipolar. In other words, while some groups do as well as whites, other groups such as Vietnamese Americans and Cambodian Americans have considerably higher poverty rates.[140]

Why Drop Out?

Just as reliable statistics on the dropout rate are difficult to obtain, precise data on the causes of dropping out—and on the reasons cited by students—are elusive and sometimes contradictory. The commonly held belief that female students drop out because they are pregnant reflects only part of the reality: 50 to 60 percent of female dropouts report leaving school for reasons other than pregnancy.[141]

Thirty-seven percent of the female dropouts compared to only 5 percent of the male dropouts in a recent study cited "family-related problems" as the reason they left high school.[142] In fact, a recent comprehensive study of research on school dropouts concludes:

"Some background characteristics associated with dropping out apply equally to girls and boys. These include low socioeconomic status, minority status, and low parental-education levels. Another set of background characteristics seem to influence more female than male dropouts. These include having a large number of siblings and mother's education level."[143]

Traditional gender roles place greater family responsibilities and strains on adolescent girls than on their brothers. Girls are often expected to "help out" with caretaking responsibilities; boys rarely encounter this expectation, although they may be expected to assist their families financially. Twenty-seven percent of male dropouts, compared to only 11 percent of female dropouts, mention work as one of the reasons for leaving school.[144] In fact, girls who drop out of school are more likely to hold traditional gender-role stereotypes than are girls who graduate. Female dropouts are more likely to believe a woman's role is in the home, not in the work force.[145]

However, girls as well as boys drop out of school simply because they do not consider school to be a pleasant or worthwhile place to spend their time. According to the Department of Education's High School and Beyond data, 82 percent of the girls who dropped out cited a school-related reason such as poor grades or dislike of school among the reasons they gave for leaving. School-related reasons were given as the primary cause for dropping out by 36 percent of white girls, 29 percent of black girls, and 21 percent of Hispanic girls.[146] Researcher Michelle Fine and her colleagues have found that often it is the most assertive girls who leave school:

> *"A moderate level of depression, an absence of political awareness, persistent self-blame, low assertiveness, and high conformity may tragically have constituted the 'good' urban student at this high school. They learned not to raise, and indeed to help shut down, 'dangerous' conversation. The price of academic 'success' may have been the muting of one's own voice."[147]*

Looking at students at the point when they leave school tells only part of the story. The early antecedents of dropping out are crucial. Repeating one or more grades in school is a strong predictor of subsequent school dropout for both boys and girls, but girls who have been held back tend to leave school even earlier than do boys. In one study, 92 percent of the girls who dropped out—but only 22 percent of the boys—tied their decision to having been held back.[148] Girls' greater sensitivity to social situations may make them more uncomfortable than their male peers in out-of-age class-rooms. In the words of one girl, "It felt real bad. First I felt so tall compared to them little ones and then my brother was in the class and so finally I left."[149]

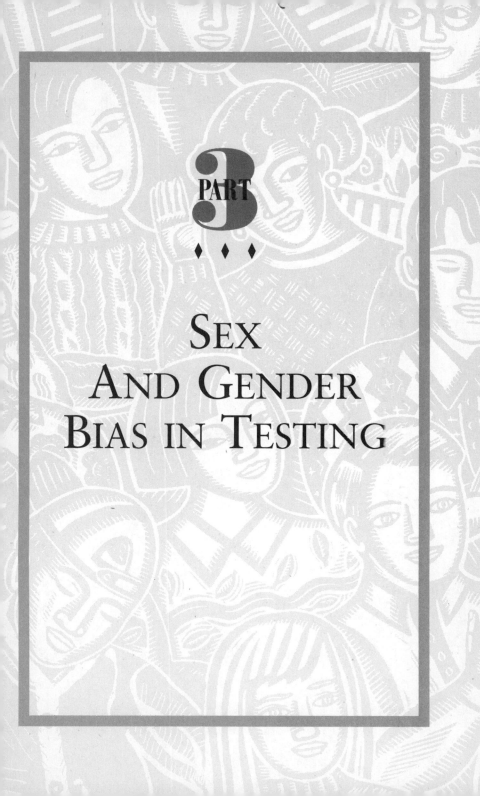

PART 3

SEX AND GENDER BIAS IN TESTING

Many of the research studies reviewed in this report use test results as key measures of outcomes. Whenever tests are used, issues of sex and gender bias must be addressed.* As this section will show, questions of sex bias in the design, construction, and administration of tests are complex. Perfectly good achievement tests can be designed in math, language arts, and other subjects on which girls will tend to score higher than boys. Other equally good tests can be developed on which boys will tend to score higher, and still other tests can be developed on which there will be no sex differences. "No sex differences" does not mean that all girls and boys will get the same scores. Rather, it means that scores will vary according to individual skills, knowledge, and motivation. However, the scores of girls *as a group* and of boys *as a group* will be about the same.

Bias in Tests

Test results are the basis of most educational research and evaluation and play a large role in research-and-

"[Testing is] overrelied upon, lacks adequate public accountability, sometimes leads to unfairness in the al ocation of opportunities, and too often undermines vital social policies."

From Gate Keepers to Gateway: Transforming Testing in America (Chestnut Hill, MA: National Commission on Testing and Public Policy, 1990), p. xi.

---

*The contribution of researchers at the Educational Testing Service (ETS) to what we know about testing and gender—and their willingness to share that data—must be acknowledged. Indeed, because of the accessibility of SAT/GRE data, it has been used so frequently in studies of gender and test bias that care should be taken in generalizing the results to other tests. In research on testing, the terms *sex* and *gender* are used interchangeably even more frequently than in other areas. This section reflects that usage.

evaluation-based policy decisions. Tests are instrumental in deciding who passes, who goes to selective colleges, and who receives scholarships.[1] While girls are more apt than boys to go to college and to get higher grades in both high school and college, scholarships based on test scores are twice as likely to go to boys.[2]

The tests discussed here are standardized tests. Teacher-made tests are not included because there is little research on them and little that can be generalized about them. The discussion on standardized tests considers, as much as possible, the interaction of sex and race/ethnicity, a linkage usually overlooked.

Much of the "test unfairness" cited by the National Commission is seen as being caused by sex and race/ethnic bias. Biased tests, those that favor one sex or one group, are specifically prohibited by Title IX of the Education Amendments of 1972. Discrimination in the use of tests is also forbidden.[3]

Title IX

While tests contribute to unfairness and discrimination, in most cases tests reflect rather than cause inequities in American education. Differences between groups are often taken as proof of test bias. But some differences "may simply mean that the groups on average know different amounts about what is being tested."[4] Particularly when issues of race/ethnicity and socioeconomic status are addressed, differences in test results often reflect differences in educational opportunities and resources.

reliability *validity*

A good test must be both reliable and valid. The reliability of a test is the extent to which it measures something consistently. The validity of a test is the extent to which it measures that which it is said to measure.

Validity is specific to a particular use and a particular situational context. In aptitude tests, the most important form of validity is predictive validity, the degree to which the test predicts future performance.

As already noted, the fact that groups score differently on a test does not necessarily mean that the test is biased. If, however, the score differences are related to the validity of the test—for example, say that girls and boys know about the same amount of math but boys' test scores are consistently and significantly higher— then the test is biased. Bias is also present when the number of references to or characters of one sex exceeds the numbers represented by the other sex or if roles are presented stereotypically.[5]

Research in this area has centered around the search for bias in individual test items. To look for bias, researchers match females and males on overall test performance and then look at test items where the gender differences are greater than on the test as a whole.

The most obvious source of bias is the number of references to women and men included in items and whether the sexes are portrayed in stereotypical ways. In the 1970s most test companies developed procedures to balance the numbers of references to women and men in their tests and to screen out items that might be offensive. However, a 1984 analysis of tests found twice as many references to men as to women, and more pictures of and references to boys than girls. Even male animals were listed almost twice as often as female animals.[6] A later study of the SAT found references to forty-two men and only three women in the reading comprehension passages used in the four 1984–85 exams. Of the forty-two men, thirty-four were famous and their work was cited; one of the three women was famous (Margaret Mead) and her work was criticized.[7] These findings indicate there has not been much of a change from Tittle, McCarthy, and Steckler's 1974 study of the roles of women and men in achievement tests.[8]

It is possible to create or eliminate sex differences in test scores in the content areas or in "intelligence" by the selection of test items. For example, the 1942 revision of the Stanford Binet test had as its aim to "produce a scale which will yield comparable I.Q.s for the sexes."[9] To do this, the authors accepted the hypothesis that large sex differences can exist in experience and training, and "sought to avoid using test items showing large sex differences in percents passing."[10] These test developers were aware that "intellect can be defined and measured in such a manner as to make either sex appear superior."[11]

The Stanford-Binet is not the only test that developers have constructed to eliminate sex differences. CTB/McGraw-Hill staff were quoted as saying that "very little bias was found in the California Achievement Test, and those questions were balanced so that an equal number of items favored each sex."[12] Similarly, researchers at the Educational Testing Service report that the SAT-Verbal reading passages were selected from different disciplines in specific percentages because of empirical evidence that this would help balance scores between the sexes.[13]

CAT balanced

Other research concludes that "while specific changes in the content of the SAT could not be associated with score changes, it seems likely that numerous small adjustments have played some part in recent shifts among the average test scores of women and men [to favor men]."[14] Researchers found that, as a result of efforts to make the SAT-Verbal more sex-neutral, the "relative slight advantage [three to ten points] has been shifted from women to men."[15] It is interesting to note that no efforts have been made to balance the SAT-Math, on which males outscore females by about one-half of a standard deviation, or about fifty points.

Tests are balanced or unbalanced by the selection of test items with different characteristics. Test items can differ in terms of

◆ that which is being tested (skill areas),

◆ the format of the item (such as essay or multiple choice),

◆ the item content and context (including the use of gender references and the selection of a reading comprehension passage on, say, child care or football).[16]

The relative emphasis placed on different skill areas within a content area determines if a test will help minimize or maximize sex differences. While much of the work in this area has been related to mathematics, the conclusions can be generalized to other areas. In mathematics, girls outperform boys in computation, while boys outperform girls in some problem solving.[17] Even when girls and boys were matched on overall skill areas, girls performed significantly better on mathematics test items that required arithmetic algebra than they did on items requiring arithmetic geometry. Girls' performance was also higher in areas of logic.[18] For the 1987 SAT, where boys outperformed girls on almost all items, the differences were smaller in arithmetic and algebra questions than in geometry questions.[19]

In general, if a mathematics test emphasizes computation, logic, and combined arithmetic-and-algebra skills, girls will do better. If the test emphasizes word problems and combined arithmetic-and-geometry skills, boys will do better. All of these areas are integral parts of mathematical knowledge, but the emphasis test developers place on one area or another area can increase or decrease gender differences.

As noted earlier, some gender differences persist in math and science course taking: boys are more apt to take physics and calculus.[20] As a result, science and math tests that include larger numbers of physics or calculus items tend to favor boys.

On SAT-Verbal items, girls tend to perform better on test material that is general and abstract rather than specific and concrete. Girls also appear to do better when asked to deal with concepts and ideas rather than facts and "things."[21]

The same skills can be tested in very different test contexts. For example, a student's ability to grasp analogies can be tested by having a question that refers to "guns:war" or "pans:dinner." The context in which skills are tested can skew test outcomes.

Generally boys outperform girls in applying mathe-

"Your high school record is probably the best single predictor of how well you will do in college, but a combination of your high school grades and test [SAT] scores is an even better indicator."

Taking the SAT, New York: College Entrance Examination Board, 1989, p. 4.

matics to measurement, sports, and science areas. Girls outperform boys in applying knowledge to areas of aesthetics, interpersonal relationships, and traditionally female tasks.[22] However, girls did not do as well as boys on SAT word problems even when the problems related to food and cooking.[23]

In verbal areas there is a consistent gender pattern in scores across the Graduate Record Examination (GRE) and the SAT. The context of most verbal items strongly favoring men relates to science or sports, while the context for verbal items strongly favoring women relates to aesthetic or philosophical areas or to relationships.[24]

The amount of science content in reading-comprehension passages on the SAT-Verbal jumped from 20 percent before 1978 to 33 percent after. By 1980, two years after the increase in science content, reading subscores favoring boys had climbed from three to twelve points.[25]

References to females and males appear less problematic, at least in one study of mathematics testing. Here, researchers found that "reference to male or female names, pronouns, possessions, or occupations in the place of neutral language had no demonstrable effect at all on examinee performance on mathematics word problems."[26] However, students of both sexes were more apt to omit problems with unfamiliar content, and less likely to solve such problems correctly. Familiarity is correlated with stereotypical content for girls but not boys.[27] Girls performed better on items that mirrored curriculum content, while boys tended to perform better on less routine, "real life" word problems.[28]

College students' scores on word problems, however,

did not consistently reflect an item's sex typing as defined by researchers. For example, a question about the amount of stuffing in a chair might have been expected to favor girls, while another about the amount of oxygen in a tank might have been expected to favor boys. However, when *students*, not researchers, defined an item as "masculine" or "feminine," the sex typing of those items made a major difference in female and male performance. Items identified as favoring women involved "batter in a loaf pan" and "a secretary typing business letters," while items identified as favoring boys involved "timing a male runner," "buying uniforms for a baseball team," and "computing sports averages."[29]

The proportion of different item types within a test can determine whether sex differences are found. Girls tend to score higher on essay or open-ended items, while boys tend to score higher on multiple-choice items.[30] There are also sex differences in the number of items completed, with girls completing fewer items. Seventh-grade girls taking the SAT and girls taking the National Assessment of Educational Progress (NAEP) science assessment are more apt than boys to respond "I don't know" and to fail to reach the end of the test.[31]

Seventh-grade girls taking the SAT-Math fared better than boys on questions about the amount of information needed to solve a problem (data sufficiency items). Predictably, they found the multiple-choice items harder. No difference was found on those items that contained figures and/or diagrams.[32]

Sex differences have been found within the different types of objective items. For example, the use of analogies slightly favors boys.[33] The use of antonyms slightly favors girls.[34] Girls and boys perform equally well on science inquiry items, where an understanding of process is key, but girls do less well when tested on specific science content.[35]

The impact of affective factors is mixed. While girls report being more anxious about tests than do boys, girls' increased anxiety does not correlate with poorer test performance.[36] Attitudes toward math do not have an impact on the SAT-Math gender gap. Sex differences in SAT-Math scores were found even among students who chose math as their favorite subject or who chose science first and math second.[37] It also appears that attitudes toward science are not central in explaining gender differences in science achievement.[38]

Perhaps most important, SAT scores, which are designed to predict college success as defined by first-year grades, underpredict women's grades and overpredict men's. Young women tend to receive higher college grades than young men with the same SAT scores.[39]

The underprediction of women's college grades does not result from women taking easier courses. In math courses at all levels, grades of females and males are very similar, but male SAT-Math scores are higher than female scores.[40] Attempts to control statistically for differences in courses taken usually diminish—but do not

> "**W**hatever other faults paper and pencil tests may have, the scanning machine is completely oblivious to the personal characteristics of the person who filled out the answer sheet. The potential for bias in the scoring of performance tests is clear. Scorers are human and fallible. Biases both for and against members of certain groups may be blatant or subtle, but they are likely to be present."
>
> M. Zieky, "Are Performance Tests for Teacher Certification Less Biased Than Paper and Pencil Tests?" Paper presented at the annual meeting of the American Educational Research Association, San Francisco, CA, April 1989.

eliminate—gender differences in over- and underprediction of grades based on SAT scores.[41] When researchers compared the SAT-Math scores of college women and men who had earned the same grades in the same college courses, they found women's scores were thirty-five points lower than those of their male classmates. The authors concluded that there may be "evidence of unfairness to women on the SAT-Math; women score lower than men of comparable academic performance."[42]

In the American College Testing Program (ACT), girls score slightly higher than boys in English and lower in math.[43] While girls earn slightly higher grades than boys in high school English courses, they earn about the same grades in math. Boys score higher than girls in math even when both have taken four years of high school math. One analysis found that female high school students had a much higher correlation between their SAT and ACT scores than do males. The SAT-Math score of a girl with an ACT math score of 20 is predicted to be 470, while the SAT-Math score of a boy with an ACT score of 20 is predicted to be 540.[44]

This has serious implications for girls and women. Test scores affect qualifications for scholarships and a variety of educational opportunities.[45] If, in the above example, a score of 500 were the cut-off point for a scholarship, the male would be eligible while the female would not.

Very little research has been conducted in the United States on bias in performance, or hands on, testing. Because research in other areas has revealed gender bias in observations, there is concern that in the new field of performance testing the scorer's observation of the examinee's age, sex, race, accent, general appearance, and mode of dress creates the potential for biased scoring.[46]

In Great Britain, studies of science performance testing at the pre-college level found that some girls chose not to do test tasks related to electricity, expressing the belief (even when that was not the case) that they did not have the necessary knowledge.[47] Some boys rejected test tasks with an obvious domestic content such as choosing the most suitable floor surface for a kitchen.[48] Furthermore, the researchers found that in some areas girls posed, and then solved, their own problems rather than doing the test task exactly as phrased by the examiner. The girls' problems were frequently more complex and required sophisticated procedural strategies to solve. However, all too often such behavior was labeled as "off task" and "incorrect" and the girls were scored down.[49]

Implications

Research shows that one result of bias in testing is that test scores may provide an inaccurate picture of girls' and boys' abilities. Other factors, such as grades, portfolios of student work, extracurricular achievements, and out-of-school accomplishments, must be considered along with test scores when making judgments about girls' and boys' skills and abilities.

PART 4

THREE PERSPECTIVES ON CURRICULUM

Section Four focuses on school curriculum from three perspectives:

♦ the Formal Curriculum, or the content of curricular materials,

♦ the Classroom As Curriculum, meaning the ways in which these materials are taught, and

♦ the Evaded Curriculum, the things that are *not* taught in our nation's schools.

The formal curriculum is the central message-giving instrument of the school. It can strengthen or decrease student motivation for engagement, effort, growth, and development through the messages it delivers to students about themselves and the world. Curricular materials that do not reflect the diversity of students' lives and cultures provide incomplete and inaccurate messages.

Research reveals that although sexism has decreased in some school texts, examples of omission, tokenism, and gender stereotyping still occur frequently in textbook references to girls and women. This is particularly unfortunate in light of research that documents the benefits of gender-equitable materials to students of both sexes.

Furthermore, whether one looks at preschool classrooms or university lecture halls, at female teachers or male teachers, research spanning the past twenty years consistently reveals that males receive more teacher attention than do females. There is also a tendency for schools to choose curricular materials that will appeal more to boys' interests. The long-term combined message of both formal curricular materials and informal classroom interaction patterns is a discouraging one for girls and young women.

This discouragement is deepened by the absence of serious attention to many daily realities of students' lives. Sexuality, violence, and physical and emotional abuse are evaded topics in schools. Furthermore, discussions of "gender politics," the unequal treatment of women and men in our society, are virtually absent in most of the nation's classrooms. Until matters of gender are considered seriously, neither girls nor boys will receive an education that is both excellent and equitable.

THE FORMAL CURRICULUM

♦

The formal curriculum is the central message-giving instrument of the school. It creates images of self and the world for all students. The curriculum can strengthen or decrease student motivation for engagement, effort, growth, and development through the messages it delivers to students about themselves and the world.

Students spend more hours of the day in academic classes than in any other activity. The chief subject areas today are basically the same as they were at the turn of the century, albeit with some changes in name: English (or language arts), history (or social studies), mathematics, science, foreign (or second) language, arts, and physical education. Accreditation of students for further education or employment depends more on grades given for curricular work in these areas than on any other formal measure.

Despite the importance of curriculum, its actual content received scant attention in national reports on education and education restructuring in the late 1980s.[1] These reports found student achievement unsatisfactory, but very few questioned whether curriculum content might in fact be counterproductive to student achievement. The reports suggest that levels of literacy, numer-

"In twelve years of school, I never studied anything about myself."

Twelfth-grade African American girl, New York–area urban high school, March 1991.

acy, and commitment to life-long learning are not satisfactory for either girls or boys in our society. Improving the situation for girls can also improve it for boys, for when one looks carefully at girls' dilemmas, boys' dilemmas are seen from new perspectives.

Yet in 138 articles on educational reform that appeared in nine prominent educational journals between 1983 and 1987, less than 1 percent of the text addressed sex equity. Only one article discussed curriculum and instruction as they relate to sex equity.[2] A 1990 survey commissioned by the National Education Association revealed that even among programs sponsored by organizations and institutions concerned with equity in education, only three national professional development programs for teachers focused on gender and race in English and social studies curriculum content.[3]

Research on Curriculum

Since the early 1970s, many studies have surveyed instructional materials for sex bias.[4] Published in 1975, *Dick and Jane As Victims: Sex Stereotyping in Children's Readers* set a pattern for line-by-line examination of the messages about girls and boys delivered by texts, examples, illustrations, and thematic organization of material in everything from basal readers to science textbooks.[5] In 1971 a study of thirteen popular U.S. history textbooks revealed that material on women comprised no more than 1 percent of any text, and that women's lives were trivialized, distorted, or omitted altogether.[6] Studies from the late 1980s reveal that although sexism has decreased in some elementary school texts and basal readers, the problems persist, especially at the secondary school level, in terms of what is considered important enough to study.[7]

A 1989 study of book-length works taught in high school English courses reports that, in a national sample of public, independent, and Catholic schools, the ten books assigned most frequently included only one written by a woman and none by members of minority groups.[8] This research, which used studies from 1963 and 1907 as a base line, concludes that "the lists of most frequently required books and authors are dominated by white males, with little change in overall balance from similar lists 25 or 80 years ago."[9]

During the late 1970s and '80s, experiments with more inclusive school curricula were aided by the rapid development of scholarly work and courses in black studies, ethnic studies, and women's studies in colleges and universities. Publications of the Council on Interracial Books for Children (founded in 1966), The Feminist Press (founded in 1970), and the federally funded Women's Educational Equity Program (started in 1974) inspired many teachers to develop more inclusive reading lists and assignments that draw on students' lives.

What effects did the revised curricula have on students? A 1980 review of research on how books influence children cited twenty-three studies that demonstrated that books do transmit values to young readers, that multicultural readings produce markedly more favorable attitudes toward nondominant groups than do all-white curricula, that academic achievement for all students was positively correlated with use of nonsexist and multicultural curriculum materials, and that

"A 1980 analysis of the twenty-four most widely used teacher-education textbooks found that less than 1 percent of the space in the texts was devoted to the problems of sexism. The authors of the study concluded that teacher education was reinforcing sex bias rather than reducing it."

M. Sadker and D. Sadker, "Sexism in Teacher Education Texts," Harvard Educational Review 50, no. 1 (February 1980): 36–46.

sex-role stereotyping was reduced in those students whose curriculum portrayed females and males in non-stereotypical roles.[10]

During the 1980s, federal support for research and action on sex equity and race equity dropped sharply.[11] But many individual teachers, librarians, authors, and local or state school authorities continued a variety of efforts to lessen stereotyping and omission, or expand and democratize the curriculum.[12]

Virtually all textbook publishers now have guidelines for nonsexist language. Unfortunately, not all insist that authors follow them.[13] Change in textbooks is observable but not striking. Research on high school social studies texts reveals that while women are more often included, they are likely to be the usual "famous women," or women in protest movements. Rarely is there dual and balanced treatment of women and men, and seldom are women's perspectives and cultures presented on their own terms.[14]

Researchers at a 1990 conference reported that even texts designed to fit within the current California guidelines on gender and race equity for textbook adoption showed subtle language bias, neglect of scholarship on women, omission of women as developers of history and initiators of events, and absence of women from accounts of technological developments.[15] An informal survey of twenty U.S. history textbooks compiled each year from 1984 to 1989 found a gradual but steady shift away from an overwhelming emphasis on laws, wars, and control over territory and public policy, toward an emphasis on people's daily lives in many kinds of circumstances.[16] The books, however, continued to maintain the abstract, disengaged tone that was characteristic of the earlier texts. The recommended assignments still relied heavily on debate techniques in which students were asked to develop an argument defending a single point of view. Few assignments offered students an opportunity to reflect on a genuine variety of perspectives or to consider feelings as well as actions.[17]

Conceptualizations of Equity in the Curriculum

Side by side with research on gender and the curriculum came various ways of conceptualizing and categorizing what is meant by gender and race equity in curriculum content. Recognizing elements of bias was an important first step. Building on earlier efforts, including work by Martha Matthews and Shirley McCune at the National Foundation for the Improvement of Education, leaders of workshops sponsored by the National Council of Teachers of Foreign Languages in 1984 listed six common forms of sex bias in instructional materials: *exclusion* of girls, *stereotyping* of members of both sexes, *subordination or degradation* of girls, *isolation* of materials on women, *superficiality* of attention to contemporary issues or social problems, and *cultural inaccuracy*, through which most of the people active in a culture are excluded from view.[18] The

> A 1985 review of more than 100 research studies concluded, "Pupils who are exposed to sex-equitable materials are more likely than others to 1) have gender-balanced knowledge of people in society, 2) develop more flexible attitudes and more accurate sex-role knowledge, and 3) imitate role behaviors contained in the material....The evidence is strong in support of using these materials to improve the learning experiences of both females and males."
>
> K. Scott and C. Schau, "Sex Equity and Sex Bias in Instructional Materials" in S. Klein, ed., Handbook for Achieving Sex Equity Through Education (Baltimore: The Johns Hopkins University Press, 1985), p. 228.

Coalition of Women in German has monitored text-books using this checklist for several years and reports significant changes in texts.[19]

In 1990, after a review of more than 100 sex- and race-equity programs identified further markers of bias in the classroom, the National Education Association developed a checklist specifying eleven kinds of sex bias. The "overt and subtle behaviors" it listed include: double standards for males and females, condescension, tokenism, denial of achieved status or authority, backlash against women who succeed in improving their status, and divide-and-conquer strategies that praise individuals as better than others in their ethnic or gender group.[20]

Unfortunately, checklists on bias, prejudice, and discrimination can sometimes hurt the very groups they are meant to help by assigning them the status of "victims." In a provocative essay, "Curriculum As Window and Mirror," Emily Style compares the curriculum to an architectural structure that schools build around students.[21] Ideally, the curriculum provides each student with both windows out onto the experiences of others and mirrors of her or his own reality and validity. But for most students, the present curriculum provides many windows and few mirrors.

Teachers themselves may recall few mirrors. For the last eleven years, teachers joining a large faculty-development project have been asked, "What did you study about women in high school?" More than half initially respond, "Nothing." Some recall a heroine, one or two historical figures, a few goddesses or saints. Marie Curie is the only female scientist who has been mentioned in ten years of this survey.[22] Many women as well as men are surprised at their answers, and surprised to realize how little they themselves are teaching about women and girls. Questions about cultural diversity draw similar responses. Virtually all teachers polled recall feeling a distance between their own lives and what was portrayed in the formal curriculum.

Curriculum researcher Gretchen Wilbur states that gender-fair curriculum has six attributes. It acknowledges and affirms *variation*, i.e., similarities and differences among and within groups of people. It is *inclusive*, allowing both females and males to find and identify positively with messages about themselves. It is *accurate*, presenting information that is data-based, verifiable, and able to withstand critical analysis. It is *affirmative*, acknowledging and valuing the worth of individuals and groups. It is *representative*, balancing multiple perspectives. And, finally, it is *integrated*, weaving together the experiences, needs, and interests of both males and females.[23]

Wilbur maintains that so far no major curriculum-reform efforts have used explicitly gender-fair approaches. For example, the National Council of Teachers of Mathematics has developed new mathematics standards that shift the emphasis of curriculum from computational skills to mastery of concepts and processes.[24] The new standards advocate 1) conceptual orientation, 2) active involvement physically and mentally, 3) thinking, reasoning, and problem solving, 4) application, 5) broad range of content, and 6) use of calculators.[25] Wilbur states that, if implemented effectively, this approach will fulfill three out of the six criteria for gender-fair content: variation, accuracy, and representation. However, there is no assurance that the curriculum will be inclusive, affirming, or integrated.

Currently, science-curriculum-reform efforts under Project 2061 of the American Association for the Advancement of Science describe equity as the central organizing principle; however, the materials produced to date send contradictory messages. For example, while acknowledging that scientific discoveries have been made around the world, the new science materials refer specifically to only European scientific history and the usual "great men." So far, women are no more visible in Project 2061 than in standard science-curriculum materials.[26]

Wilbur categorizes many attempts to design gender-fair courses as *pullout* curricula, which target a "problem" population (for example, pregnant teenagers or persons with disabilities), or *fragmented* curricula, which add units on "women's issues" to the main curriculum. Such approaches, she maintains, fall short of genuinely gender-fair integration of women into central course content.

These and other kinds of corrective programs have been noted by other educators. James Banks identifies four ways in which ethnic content has been integrated into the curriculum since the 1960s. He describes these ways, or "levels," as follows.

Level 1: The Contributions Approach	Focuses on heroes, holidays, and discrete cultural elements.
Level 2: The Additive Approach	Content, concepts, themes, and perspectives are added to the curriculum without changing its structure.

Level 3: The Trans-formation Approach	The structure of the curriculum is changed to enable students to view concepts, issues, events, and themes from the perspectives of diverse ethnic and cultural groups.
Level 4: The Social Action Approach	Students make decisions on important social issues and take actions to help solve them.[27]

In another typology, Peggy McIntosh identifies five interactive phases of curricular and personal change that she observed in educators trying to teach more inclusively than they were themselves taught. The following analysis, which uses history as an example, applies to all subject areas. McIntosh describes Phase I as "Womanless and All-White History." Phase II is "Exceptional Women and Persons of Color in History," but only considered from the conventional perspective of, for instance, military, political, or publicly acknowledged leaders. Phase III she terms the "Issues" Curriculum, treating "Women and People of Color as Problems, Anomalies, Absences, or Victims in History." Phases I, II, and III have a vertical axis of "either/or thinking" that views winning and losing as the only alternatives. An important conceptual and emotional shift occurs in Phase IV, which she labels "Women's Lives or the Lives of People of Color *As* History." In Phase IV, which features lateral and plural thinking, we see, for the first time, the cyclical nature of daily life, the making and mending of the social fabric, which was projected onto "lower-caste" people. This phase, when interactively explored with the other phases, makes possible the eventual reconstruction of Phase V, "History Redefined and Reconstructed to Include Us All."[28]

Many school subjects, as presently taught, fall within the general descriptions of Phases I and II. In the upper grades especially, the curriculum narrows and definitions of knowing take on gender-specific and culture-specific qualities associated with Anglo-European male values.[29] For example, current events and civics curricula, which take up topics from the news media, tend to focus, like their sources, on news as controversy and conflict. Much of the daily texture of life is ignored in most current-events classes.[30]

Debate clubs, usually located at the boundary of the formal curriculum as an extracurricular activity, take for granted the adversarial, win/lose orientation of debate. The definition of the citizen in debate clubs and current-events classes relates more to what psychologist Carol Gilligan names "the ethos of justice" (negotiating rights and responsibilities) than to "the ethos of care" (working relationally to make and keep human connections and avoid damage).[31]

Over the last forty years, most educators have assumed that the existing subject areas of the curriculum serve a useful purpose. They are in such universal use that consideration of alternatives is difficult. They are viewed as providing a rational educational grounding, especially in preparation for standardized tests such as College Board or Regents' Exams in individual subject areas. Increasingly, however, educational organizations, colleges, and testing agencies themselves are acknowledging the importance of students' gaining the ability not only to describe concepts but to apply them in new situations. Traditional discipline-based courses, while providing factual information, may not be the best way to do this.

Changing the curriculum in any substantial way is bound to result in some initial resistance. A recent study commissioned by the National Education Association identified several key barriers to gender equity in the curriculum. The report cited students' reluctance to be singled out as having cultural or gender experience that does not fit the assumed norms; parents' suspicions about unfamiliar curricula; teachers' lack of training on multicultural and gender-neutral goals and techniques; unwillingness to commit funds for teachers to participate in curriculum-change efforts.[32]

School systems often lack in-service funds and energy to provide new opportunities for teachers. Tracy Kidder's noted study of a year in the life of a fourth-grade teacher, *Among School Children*, notes that the teacher uses twenty-year-old curriculum guides.[33]

Arthur Applebee, author of the noted *Study of Book-Length Works Taught in High School English Courses*, says that twenty years of consciousness raising and resource development have not changed the basic curriculum because teachers have not had the time and support to familiarize themselves with new materials. He recommends preservice course work in schools of education, in-service workshops, and departmental discussion groups to give teachers enough familiarity with alternative materials so that they will be comfortable in finding their own ways to introduce new works into their classes.[34] The restructuring of schools should acknowledge that curricular design and revision are central—not peripheral—to teachers' work with students.

The Multicultural Debate

The most important impediment to gender-fair and multicultural curricula may be inherited views of what education is and whom it should serve. For example, when it became clear that New York's schools were not serving the population well, New York Commissioner of Education Thomas Sobol created a committee for the review and development of Social Studies curricula in the schools. The committee's report is a clear commitment to curricular principles of democracy, diversity, economic and social justice, globalism, ecological balance, ethics and values, and the individual and society.[35] It recommends that curriculum and teaching methods be more inclusive and respectful of diversity. The report has created a furor in the New York media, reflecting the larger debate going on throughout the country. Critics have called Ethnic Studies and Women's Studies "political," as if a curriculum that leaves women out altogether is not also "political." Multicultural work has been termed "divisive" without recognizing that an exclusively white male curriculum is divisive when it ignores the contri-

> *Across the whole spectrum of the K–12 curriculum there is currently more emphasis on the development of assertive than affiliative skills, more reward for solo behavior than collaborative behavior, more reward for speaking than for listening. The curriculum can be strengthened by consciously focusing on the development of reflective, caring, collaborative skills as well as those skills emphasizing individual performance and achievement.*

butions others make to society. Critics who insist that students must focus on our "common heritage" appear to overlook the experiences of Native Americans as well as the immigrant history of the rest of the population, which makes diversity one of the key elements of the "common" heritage of the United States.

In a democracy, schools must address the educational needs of all students. Each student should find herself or himself reflected in the curriculum. When this happens, students learn and grow.

Girls, Self-Esteem, and the Curriculum

Researchers have puzzled over the drop in girls' self-esteem as they go through school, even though they do as well as boys on many standardized measures and get better grades. Teacher trainer Cathy Nelson attributes this drop in self-esteem to the negative messages delivered to girls by school curricula.[36] Students sit in classes that, day in and day out, deliver the message that women's lives count for less than men's. Historian Linda Kerber suggests a plausible connection between falling self-esteem and curricular omission and bias. "Lowered self-esteem is a perfectly reasonable conclusion if one has been subtly instructed that what people like oneself have done in the world has not been important and is not worth studying."[37] There is no social science research to document cause and effect in this matter, but educators must take more responsibility for understanding that the curriculum is the central message-giving instrument of the school.

THE CLASSROOM AS
CURRICULUM

◆

"Learning is enhanced when students understand what is expected of them, get recognition for their work, learning about their errors and receiving guidance in improving their performance."

J. Goodlad, *A Place Called School: Prospects for the Future* (New York, 1984), p. 111.

Students can learn as much from what they experience in school as they can from the formal content of classroom assignments. Classroom interactions, both with the teacher and other students, are critical components of education. These interactions shape a school. They determine in large measure whether or not a school becomes a community: a place where girls and boys can learn to value themselves and others, where both the rights and the responsibilities of citizens are fostered.

Teacher-Student Interactions

Whether one looks at preschool classrooms or university lecture halls, at female teachers or male teachers, research spanning the past twenty years consistently reveals that males receive more teacher attention than do females.[1] In preschool classrooms boys receive more instructional time, more hugs, and more teacher attention.[2] The pattern persists through elementary school and high school. One reason is that boys demand more attention. Researchers David and Myra Sadker have studied these patterns for many years. They report that boys in one study of elementary and middle school students called out answers significantly more often than girls did. When boys called out, the typical teacher reaction was to listen to the comment. When girls called out, they were usually corrected with comments such as, "Please raise your hand if you want to speak."[3]

The issue is broader than the inequitable distribution of teacher *contacts* with male and female students; it also includes the inequitable *content* of teacher comments. Teacher remarks can be vague and superficial or precise and penetrating. Helpful teacher comments provide students with insights into the strengths and weaknesses of their answers. Careful and comprehensive teacher reactions not only affect student learning, they can also influence student self-esteem.[4]

The Sadkers conducted a three-year study of more than 100 fourth-, sixth- and eighth-grade classrooms. They identified four types of teacher comments: praise, acceptance, remediation, and criticism.

They found that while males received more of all four types of teacher comments, the difference favoring boys was greatest in the more useful teacher reactions of praise, criticism, and remediation. When teachers took the time and made the effort to specifically evaluate a student's performance, the student receiving the comment was more likely to be male.[5] These findings are echoed in other investigations, indicating that boys receive more precise teacher comments than females in terms of both scholarship and conduct.[6]

The differences in teacher evaluations of male and female students have been cited by some researchers as a cause of "learned helplessness," or lack of academic perseverance, in females. Initially investigated in animal experiments, "learned helplessness" refers to a lack of

An Approach to Change

In *Kentucky, the Office of Technical Education in the Cabinet for Workforce Development has undertaken an intensive research and training project. Trained observers watched and coded 245 randomly selected vocational-education class sessions at the secondary and postsecondary levels. The results showed that males consistently received a disproportionate number of teacher comments and that the male/female disparity was even greater in high school classrooms than it was at the post-secondary level. Neither the sex of the teacher nor the number of years of teaching experience affected this pattern. However, training in classroom-interaction strategies did affect teacher behavior: teachers with training provided a more equitable classroom environment.[1]*

Based on these results, the Office of Technical Education is continuing to support training sessions for teachers, and teachers themselves are telling others about what they have learned. "I hope that over a five-year period every school district and every vocational school in the state will be aware of the difference teachers make in their classes. I believe a good portion of the teachers will change their teaching techniques."

—Betty Tipton, Director, Equal Vocational Education Programs, Kentucky.

[1] State of Kentucky, Department of Education, Office of Vocational Education, *Teacher/Student Classroom Interaction in Vocational Education: A Sex Bias/Sex Stereotyping Project.*

perseverance, a debilitating loss of self-confidence.[7] This concept has been used to explain why girls sometimes abandon while boys persistently pursue academic challenges for which both groups are equally qualified.[8]

One school of thought links learned helplessness with attribution theory. While girls are more likely to attribute their success to luck, boys are more likely to attribute their success to ability. As a result of these different causal attributions, boys are more likely to feel mastery and control over academic challenges, while girls are more likely to feel powerless in academic situations.[9]

Studies also reveal that competent females have higher expectations of failure and lower self-confidence when encountering new academic situations than do males with similar abilities.[10] The result is that female students are more likely to abandon academic tasks.[11]

However, research also indicates that the concepts of learned helplessness and other motivation constructs are complex. Psychologist Jacquelynne Eccles and her colleagues have found that there is a high degree of variation within each individual in terms of motivational constructs as one goes across subject areas. New evidence indicates that it is too soon to state a definitive connection between a specific teacher behavior and a particular student outcome.[12] Further research on the effects of teacher behavior and student performance and motivation is needed.

The majority of studies on teacher-student interaction do not differentiate among subject areas. However, there is some indication that the teaching of certain subjects may encourage gender-biased teacher behavior while others may foster more equitable interactions. Sex differences in attributing success to luck versus effort are more likely in subject areas where teacher responses are less frequent and where single precise student responses are less common.[13]

Two recent studies find teacher-student interactions in science classes particularly biased in favor of boys.[14] Some mathematics classes have less biased patterns of interaction overall when compared to science classes, but there is evidence that despite the more equitable overall pattern, a few male students in each mathematics class receive particular attention to the exclusion of all other students, male and female.[15]

Research on teacher-student interaction patterns has rarely looked at the interaction of gender with race, ethnicity, and/or social class. The limited data available indicate that while males receive more teacher attention than females, white boys receive more attention than boys from various racial and ethnic minority groups.[16]

Evidence also suggests that the attention minority students receive from teachers may be different in nature from that given to white children. In elementary school, black boys tend to have fewer interactions overall with teachers than other students and yet they are the recipients of four to ten times the amount of qualified praise ("That's good, but...") as other students.[17] Black boys tend to be perceived less favorably by their teachers and seen as less able than other students.[18] The data are more complex for girls. Black girls have less interaction with teachers than white girls, but they attempt to initiate interaction much more often than white girls or than boys of either race. Research indicates that teachers may unconsciously rebuff these black girls, who eventually turn to peers for interaction, often becoming the class enforcer or go-between for other students.[19] Black females also receive less reinforcement from teachers than do other students, although their academic performance is often better than boys'.[20]

In fact, when black girls do as well as white boys in school, teachers attribute their success to hard work but assume that the white boys are not working up to their full potential.[21] This, coupled with the evidence that blacks are more often reinforced for their social behavior while whites are likely to be reinforced for their academic accomplishments, may contribute to low academic self-esteem in black girls.[22] Researchers have found that black females value their academic achievements less than black males in spite of their better performance.[23] Another study found that black boys have a higher science self-concept than black girls although there were no differences in achievement.[24]

The Design of Classroom Activities

Research studies reveal a tendency beginning at the preschool level for schools to choose classroom activities that will appeal to boys' interests and to select presentation formats in which boys excel or are encouraged more than are girls.[25] For example, when researchers looked at lecture versus laboratory classes, they found that in lecture classes teachers asked males academically related questions about 80 percent more often than they questioned females; the patterns were mixed in laboratory classes.[26] However, in science courses, lecture classes remain more common than laboratory classes.

Research indicates that if pupils begin working on an activity with little introduction from the teacher, everyone has access to the same experience. Discussion that follows

Boys and girls view academic failure very differently. Boys often attribute their failures to lack of trying and feel that more effort is needed to be successful. Girls are more likely to attribute their failures to a simple lack of ability.

after all students have completed an activity encourages more participation by girls.[27] In an extensive multistate study, researchers found that in geometry classes where the structure was changed so that students read the book and did problems *first* and *then* had classroom discussion of the topic, girls outperformed boys in two of five tests and scored equally in the other three. Girls in the experimental class reversed the general trend of boys' dominance on applications, coordinates, and proof taking, while they remained on par with boys on visualizations in three dimensions and transformations. In traditional classes where topics were introduced by lecture first and then students read the book and did the problems, small gender differences favoring boys remained.[28]

Successful Teaching Strategies

There are a number of teaching strategies that can promote more gender-equitable learning environments. Research indicates that science teachers who are successful in encouraging girls share several strategies.[29] These included using more than one textbook, eliminating sexist language, and showing fairness in their treatment and expectations of both girls and boys.

Other research indicates that classrooms where there are no gender differences in math are "girl friendly," with less social comparison and competition and an atmosphere students find warmer and fairer.[30]

In their 1986 study, *Women's Ways of Knowing*, Belenky, Clinchy, Goldberger, and Tarule point out that for many girls and women, successful learning takes place in an atmosphere that enables students to empathetically enter into the subject they are studying, an approach the authors term "connected knowing." The authors suggest that an acceptance of each individual's personal experiences and perspectives facilitates students' learning. They argue for classrooms that emphasize collaboration and provide space for exploring diversity of opinion.[31]

Few classrooms foster "connected learning," nor are the majority of classrooms designed to encourage cooperative behaviors and collaborative efforts. The need to evaluate, rank, and judge students can undermine collaborative approaches. One recent study that sampled third-, fifth-, and seventh-grade students found that successful students reported fewer cooperative attitudes than did unsuccessful students. In this study the effects of gender varied as a function of grade level. Third-grade girls were more cooperative than their male peers, but by fifth grade the gender difference had disappeared.[32] Other studies do not report this grade level–gender interaction, but rather indicate that girls tend to be more cooperative than boys but that cooperative attitudes decline for all students as they mature.[33]

Some educators view the arrival of new classroom organizational structures as a harbinger of more effective and more equitable learning environments. "Cooperative learning" has been viewed as one of these

> **A** *study of science classes found that when teachers needed assistance in carrying out a demonstration, 79 percent of the demonstrations were carried out by boys. Science classrooms are often dominated by boys in part because boys have more extensive out-of-school familiarity and experience with the subject matter.*
>
> K. Tobin and P. Garnett, "Gender Related Differences in Science Activities," *Science Education* 71 (1987):91–103; J. Kahle, "Why Girls Don't Know," in *What Research Says to the Science Teacher—the Process of Knowing*, ed. M. Rowe (Washington, DC: National Science Testing Association, 1990)

potentially more successful educational strategies. Cooperative learning is designed to eliminate the negative effects of classroom competition while promoting a cooperative spirit and increasing heterogeneous and cross-race relationships. Smaller cooperative work groups are designed to promote group cohesion and interdependence, and mobilize these positive feelings to achieve academic objectives.[34] Progress and academic performance are evaluated on a group as well as an individual basis; the group must work together efficiently or all its members will pay a price.[35] A number of positive results have been attributed to cooperative learning groups, including increasing cross-race friendships, boosting academic achievement, mainstreaming students with disabilities, and developing mutual student concerns.[36]

However, positive cross-sex relationships may be more difficult to achieve than cross-race friendships or positive relationships among students with and without disabilities. First, as reported earlier in this report, there is a high degree of sex-segregation and same-sex friendships in elementary and middle school years.[37] Researchers have found that the majority of elementary students preferred single-sex work groups.[38] Second, different communication patterns of males and females can be an obstacle to effective cross-gender relationships. Females are more indirect in speech, relying often on questioning, while more direct males are more likely to make declarative statements or even to interrupt.[39] Research indicates that boys in small groups are more likely to receive requested help from girls; girls' requests, on the other hand, are more likely to be ignored by the boys.[40] In fact, the male sex may be seen as a status position within the group. As a result, male students may choose to show their social dominance by not readily talking with females.[412]

Not only are the challenges to cross-gender cooperation significant, but cooperative learning as currently implemented may not be powerful enough to overcome these obstacles. Some research indicates that the infrequent use of small, unstructured work groups is not effective in reducing gender stereotypes, and, in fact, increases stereotyping. Groups often provide boys with leadership opportunities that increase their self-esteem. Females are often seen as followers and are less likely to want to work in mixed-sex groups in the future.[42] Another study indicates a decrease in female achievement when females are placed in mixed-sex groups.[43] Other research on cooperative education programs has reported more positive results.[44] However, it is clear that merely providing an occasional group learning experience is not the answer to sex and gender differences in classrooms.

Problems in Student Interactions

The ways students treat each other during school hours is an aspect of the informal learning process, with significant negative implications for girls. There is mounting evidence that boys do not treat girls well. Reports of student sexual harassment—the unwelcome verbal or physical conduct of a sexual nature imposed by one individual on another—among junior high school and high school peers are increasing. In the majority of cases a boy is harassing a girl.[45]

Incidents of sexual harassment reveal as much about power and authority as they do about sexuality; the person being harassed usually is less powerful than the person doing the harassing. Sexual harassment is prohibited under Title IX, yet sex-biased peer interactions appear to be permitted in schools, if not always approved. Rather than viewing sexual harassment as serious misconduct, school authorities too often treat it as a joke.

When boys line up to "rate" girls as they enter a room, when boys treat girls so badly that they are reluctant to enroll in courses where they may be the only female, when boys feel it is good fun to embarrass girls to the point of tears, it is no joke. Yet these types of behaviors are often viewed by school personnel as harmless instances of "boys being boys."

The clear message to both girls and boys is that girls are not worthy of respect and that appropriate behavior for boys includes exerting power over girls—or over other, weaker boys. Being accused of being in any way like a woman is one of the worst insults a boy can receive. As one researcher recently observed:

> "It is just before dismissal time and a group of very active fourth-graders are having trouble standing calmly in line as they wait to go to their bus. Suddenly one of the boys grabs another's hat, runs to the end of the line, and involves a number of his buddies in a game of keep-away. The boy whose hat was taken leaps from his place in line, trying to intercept it from the others, who, as they toss it back and forth out of his reach, taunt him by yelling, 'You woman! You're a woman!' When the teacher on bus duty notices, she tells the boys that they all have warnings for not waiting in line prop-

erly. The boys resume an orderly stance but continue to mutter names—'Woman!' 'Am not.' 'Yes, you are.'—under their breath."

Margaret Stubbs, October 1990

Harassment related to sexual orientation or sexual preference has received even less attention as an equity issue than heterosexual sexual harassment.[46] Yet, examples of name calling that imply homophobia, such as "sissy," "queer," "gay," "lesbo," are common among students at all levels of schooling. The fourth-grade boys who teased a peer by calling him a "woman" were not only giving voice to the sex-role stereotype that women are weaker than and therefore inferior to men; they were also challenging their peer's "masculinity" by ascribing feminine characteristics to him in a derogatory manner. Such attacks often prevent girls, and sometimes boys, from participating in activities and courses that are traditionally viewed as appropriate for the opposite sex.

When schools ignore sexist, racist, homophobic, and violent interactions between students, they are giving tacit approval to such behaviors. Environments where students do not feel accepted are not environments where effective learning can take place.

"Sexual harassment occurs in the mundane, daily matters of school life: in the chemistry lab as well as in the carpentry shop, in the driver's ed car, and on the practice fields of extracurricular sports. Yet, despite its frequency, sexual harassment is rarely reported, tallied, investigated, or systematically documented."

Dr. Nan Stein, Massachusetts Department of Education.

Implications

....

Teachers are not always aware of the ways in which they interact with students. Videotaping actual classrooms so that teachers can see themselves in action can help them to develop their own strategies for fostering gender-equitable education. The use of equitable teaching strategies should be one of the criteria by which teaching performance is evaluated.

Research studies indicate that girls often learn and perform better in same-sex work groups than they do in mixed-sex groupings. Additional research is needed, however, to better understand the specific dynamics of these interactions, particularly the circumstances under which single-sex groupings are most beneficial. Single-sex classes are illegal under Title IX, but usually single-sex work groups within coed classes are not. Teachers should be encouraged to "try out" many different classroom groupings, not only in mathematics and science classes but across a wide range of subject matter. It is critical that they carefully observe the impact of various groupings and write up and report their findings.

THE EVADED CURRICULUM

♦

The evaded curriculum is the term coined in this report for matters central to the lives of students and teachers but touched upon only briefly, if at all, in most schools. These matters include the functioning of bodies, the expression and valuing of feelings, and the dynamics of power. In both formal course work and in the informal exchanges among teachers and students, serious consideration of these areas is avoided. When avoidance is not possible—as in the case of required health or sex-education courses—the material is often presented in a cursory fashion. Students are offered a set of facts devoid of references to the complex personal and moral dilemmas they face in understanding and making decisions about critical facets of their lives.

Youth is traditionally seen as a time of healthy bodies and carefree minds, but as numerous studies, reports, and television documentaries have outlined recently, young people in the United States are falling prey to what are being called the "new morbidities." These new morbidities are not necessarily caused by viruses or bacteria but rather by societal conditions that can lead young people into eating disorders, substance abuse, early sexual activity, unintended pregnancy, sexually transmitted diseases (including AIDS), and suicide.

The health and well-being of young people are related to their ability to complete school.

Not only are many young people engaging in risky behaviors, frequently with lifetime consequences, but they are taking part in constellations of behaviors that are interrelated.[1] Young people who drink, for example, are far more likely than others to engage in unprotected sex or be involved in car accidents. Girls who are doing badly in school are five times as likely as others to become teen parents.[2] It is estimated that about one-quarter of all adolescents engage in multiple problem behaviors, often with devastating consequences.[3]

While the exact demographic makeup of the highest-risk groups is not known, data on separate risk behaviors indicate that there are more young males than females at high risk. When the different patterns of risk behavior are considered, however, it becomes clear that in some areas girls are at higher risk than their male classmates.

The health and well-being of young people are related to their ability to complete school.[4] It is obvious that girls who use drugs or liquor, suffer from depression, become pregnant, or give birth as teenagers cannot take full advantage of the educational programs presented them.

Substance Use

The initial use of harmful substances is occurring at younger ages than ever before. A recent survey showed that among the 1987 high school class, significant numbers of students first tried alcohol and drugs during elementary and middle school. Two out of three students using cigarettes began smoking before the ninth grade, and one out of four first used marijuana before the ninth grade. One out of twenty students who used cocaine used it before entering ninth grade.[5]

Differences between male and female patterns of reported drug use have declined over the past two decades to the point where researchers no longer consider the sex of an adolescent a good predictor of drug use.[6] One report states that "girls are more like boys in use of substances during adolescence than at any time later in life."[7] There are some sex differences in use patterns, however. Girls are more likely to use stimulants and over-the-counter weight-reduction pills, while boys are slightly more likely to report higher levels of illicit-drug use and episodes of binge drinking.[8] White high school students are more than twice as likely as black students to smoke cigarettes, and more white females are frequent smokers than students from any other sex/race group.[9]

Sexual Activity/Contraceptive Use

Initiation of sexual activity is also occurring at younger ages. Recent reports state that at least 28 percent of adolescents are sexually active by their fourteenth birthday; the average age at the initiation of sexual activity for this group is 12.[10] A recent survey from the Alan Guttmacher Institute indicates that 38 percent of girls between the ages of fifteen and seventeen are sexually active—a 15 percent increase since 1973.[11] There has been a dramatic increase in the numbers of sexually active teenage girls who are white or from higher-income families, reducing previous racial and income differences.[12]

Contraceptive use for adolescents remains erratic,

DOES SEX EDUCATION TEACH WHAT
GIRLS NEED TO KNOW?

Sex-education courses are particularly unenlightening about girls' physical and sexual development. Typically, the courses ignore female genital development and sexual response, often presenting the male body as the "norm."[1] For girls with physical disabilities, the absence of any mention of their particular circumstances, and indeed the too-often-made assumption that they are not sexual beings, further complicates the development of a positive sense of self. Even discussion of menstruation is inadequate and has been criticized as little more than a reinforcement of the menstrual taboo, to the extent that it treats menstruation as a hygienic crisis, emphasizes negative rather than positive aspects of the cycle, fails to address girls' psychosocial concerns about menstruation, and relies predominantly on a sex-segregated format.[2] All of these aspects combine to create an association of shame rather than pride with this aspect of female development.[3]

In early adolescence girls feel particularly vulnerable to boys teasing about menstruation.[4] When menstrual education is provided only for girls, the stage is set for suspicion rather than understanding between the sexes. With a limited forum in which to ask their questions and limited guidance about appropriate responses from either adults or female peers, boys express inappropriate responses that can be cruel and harassing to girls.

Even though girls may not want boys, fathers, or brothers to know about their particular menstruation, girls do wish boys knew more about menstruation in general.[5] The availability of more inclusive teaching about menstruation within the

(continued from previous page)

school setting might broaden boys' understanding, discourage their teasing, and make school more comfortable for girls.

[1] E. Breit and M. Myerson, "Social Dimensions of the Menstrual Taboo and the Effects on Female Sexuality," in *Psychology of Women: Selected Readings,* ed. J. Williams (New York: Norton, 1979); M. Fine, "Sexuality, Schooling, and Adolescent Females: The Missing Discourse of Desire," *Harvard Educational Review* 58 (1988): 29–53; J. Rury, "We Teach the Girl Repression, the Boy Expression: Sexuality, Sex Equity and Education in Historical Perspective," *Peabody Journal of Education* 64 (1989: 44–58); M. Whatley, "Goals for Sex Equitable Education," *Peabody Journal of Education* 64 (1989): 5970.

[2] Breit and Myerson, "Social Dimensions"; L. Whisnant, "E. Brett, and L. Zegas, "Implicit Messages Concerning Menstruation in Commercial Educational Materials Prepared for Young Girls," *American Journal of Psychiatry* 132 (1975): 15–20; M. Stubbs, J. Rierdan, and E. Koff, "Becoming a Woman: Considerations in Educating Adolescents and Menstruation," Working Paper No. 160 (Wellesley, MA: Wellesley College Center for Research on Women, 1989); M. Stubbs, *Sex Education and Sex Stereotypes: Theory and Practice*, Working Paper No. 198 (Wellesley, MA: Wellesley College Center for Research on Women, 1989); J. Rierdan, E. Koff, and J. Flaherty, "Conception and Misconceptions of Menstruation," *Women and Health* 10 (1985): 33–45; "M. Stubbs, *Bodytalk* (Wellesley, MA: Wellesley College Center for Research on Women, 1990).

[3] Breit and Myerson, "Social Dimensions": Stubbs; *Bodytalk*.

[4] Stubbs, *Sex Education and Sex Stereotypes.*

[5] B. Havens and I. Swenson, "Menstrual Perceptions and Preparation among Female Adolescents," *Journal of Obstetric, Gynecologic and Neonatal Nursing* 15 (1986): 406–11.

and age is a significant factor, with younger adolescents using contraception far less frequently. Reasons adolescents give for not using contraception include (1) inadequate knowledge (both boys and girls state that they are not at risk of becoming involved in a pregnancy if they have unprotected sex), (2) lack of access to birth control, and (3) not liking to plan to have sex.[13]

Before age fifteen, only 31 percent of sexually active girls report using contraceptives. By age fifteen, only 58 percent report contraceptive use; but by age nineteen, 91 percent report that they use contraceptives.[14] Meanwhile, there is some preliminary evidence that condom use is increasing; among seventeen-to-nineteen-year-old males in metropolitan areas, reports of condom use at last intercourse more than doubled in the last decade—from 21 percent in 1979 to 58 percent in 1988.[15] Because of increased condom use, the proportion of teens using contraception at first intercourse rose from half to two-thirds between 1982 and 1988.[16] Unprotected sexual intercourse can result in too-early childbearing, discussed in detail earlier in this report. It can also result in sexually transmitted diseases (STDs).

Sexually Transmitted Diseases

Syphilis rates are equal for boys and girls, but more adolescent females than males contract gonorrhea.[17]

More than 1 million teens each year suffer from chlamydia infections, the most common STD among adolescents. Researchers speculate that teenage girls suffer high rates of STDs because the female reproductive system is particularly vulnerable during the early teen years.[18]

Nearly 715 teenagers age thirteen to nineteen have diagnosed cases of AIDS.[19] The number with HIV infection, which normally precedes AIDS, is much higher.

"Rates of physical and emotional abuse for boys and girls are very similar, but rates of sexual abuse are four times higher for girls, and their abusers are overwhelmingly male."

J. Gans and D. Blyth, *America's Adolescents: How Healthy Are They?* (Chicago: American Medical Association, 1990), p. 20.

The HIV infection rate for teenage girls is comparable to, and in some cases higher than, that for boys. While among adults, male AIDS cases are nine times more prevalent than female cases, the pattern of HIV infection among adolescents is very different. A 1989 study in the District of Columbia reports the HIV infection rate at 4.7 per 1,000 for girls, almost three times the 1.7 rate for boys.[20]

Other researchers who have been following the incidence of AIDS nationally state that teenage girls between thirteen and nineteen represent 24.9 percent of reported cases among females.[21] Women make up the fastest-growing group of persons with AIDS in the United States. The Centers for Disease Control (CDC) acknowledges that the number of reported cases is probably underestimated by 40 percent and the undercounting of women is probably more severe than for other groups because many of their symptoms are not listed in the CDC surveillance definition.[22]

Furthermore, there are differences in how AIDS is transmitted between men and women. Many more women (32.7 percent) than men (2.3 percent) become infected through a heterosexual contact; more women than men also contract AIDS through intravenous drug use.[23]

Body Image/Eating Disorders

Girls are much less satisfied with their bodies than are boys and report eating disorders at far higher rates. For example, more girls than boys report food bingeing and chronic dieting. They are also more likely to report vomiting to control their weight.[24] Severe cases of bulimia (binge eating followed by forced vomiting) and anorexia nervosa (the refusal to maintain an adequate body weight) can cause death.

Depression

An important longitudinal research study recently noted evidence of increasingly early onset and high prevalence of depression in late adolescence, with slightly more girls than boys scoring in the high range of depressive symptomology. One of the most striking findings of the study is that severely depressed girls had higher rates of substance abuse than did similarly depressed boys. Significant gender differences were found in school performance measures among the most depressed students. Grade point averages were lower for girls, and 40 percent more girls failed a grade than boys.[25]

Suicide

Adolescent girls are four to five times more likely than boys to attempt suicide (although boys are more likely to die because they choose more lethal methods, for example guns rather than sleeping pills).

A recent survey of eighth- and tenth-graders found girls are twice as likely as boys to report feeling sad and hopeless. This is consistent with clinical literature, which shows that females have higher rates of depression than males, during both adolescence and adulthood.[26]

Cohesive families, neighborhoods with adequate resources, caring adults, and quality schools all help protect teens.[27] But because the dangers they face result from a complex web of interactive social conditions and behaviors, there can be no single solution. For any program to succeed in reducing risks to teens, policymakers at every level must recognize that the needs and circumstances of girls and young women often differ from those of boys and young men.

The Functioning of Healthy Bodies

In spite of reports indicating strong public support for sex education in the schools and an increase in the number of sex-education programs offered, sex education is neither widespread nor comprehensive.[28] Few schools include sex education in the early grades, and most middle and junior high schools offer short programs of ten hours or less. It has been estimated that fewer than 10 percent of all students take comprehensive sex-education courses, i.e., courses of more than forty hours or courses designed as components within a K–12 developmental-health or sex-education program.[29]

For most teachers, knowledge of human sexuality is largely a matter of personal history rather than informed study.[30] Such knowledge is often based on traditional male-defined views of human sexuality, including unexamined gender-role-stereotyped beliefs about sexual behavior. Knowledge about sexual development is usually limited, regardless of whether the teacher is male or female.

The content of sex-education classes varies from locale to locale, in part because program planners must address local sensitivities.[31] One of the few carefully controlled field studies on sexuality- and contraceptive-education programs recently compared the impact of a special sex-education class on thirteen-to-nineteen-year-old males and females.[32] The findings indicate that publicly funded sexuality- and contraceptive-education programs as brief as eight to twelve hours appear to help participants increase their knowledge, initiate effective contraceptive use, and improve the consistent use of effective contraceptive methods by both girls and boys.

The experimental intervention appears to have been most helpful for males with prior sexual experience, improving the consistency of their use of effective methods of contraception. Females without prior sexual experience seemed to respond better to traditional sex-education programs; researchers hypothesize that the girls may have been uncomfortable with the structured, interactive, and confrontational aspects of the experimental program. The study also found that prior experience with sex education was an important predictor of contraceptive efficiency, suggesting that formal sexuality education may be an incremental learning process whose efforts may not be evident on short-term follow-up.

The absence of adequate instruction and discussion about menstruation and contraception is only a piece of the problem. The alarming increases in STDs and HIV

> The assumption of heterosexuality is a form of discrimination that is rarely discussed but that has an indelible impact on the roughly 10 percent of our youth who are homosexual or bisexual. By never raising the issue of sexual orientation as a legitimate developmental issue, by not placing informative and nonpejorative books in the school library, and by not seriously confronting homophobia in the classrooms schools abdicate their responsibility not only to adolescents who are questioning their individual sexual orientation but to all students. Homosexual girls and boys face many of the same difficulties, but lesbian students—like girls in general—are more often invisible. The few discussions of homosexuality that do occur tend to focus on gay men.

infection among adolescents, the increase in childbearing among young teens, and the increase in eating disorders make the lack of comprehensive courses on sexuality, health, and the human body unacceptable. An understanding of one's body is central to an understanding of self. The association of sexuality and health instruction exclusively with danger and disease belies the human experience of the body as a source of pleasure, joy, and comfort. Schools must take a broader, more comprehensive approach to education about growth and sexuality. An awareness that relationships with others and the development of intimacy involve both the body and the mind should be critical components of these courses.

The Expression and Valuing of Feelings

By insisting on a dichotomy between feelings and emotions on the one hand, and logic and rationality on the other, schools shortchange all students. Classrooms must become places where girls and boys can express feelings and discuss personal experiences. The lessons we learn best are those that answer our own questions. Students must have an opportunity to explore the world as they see it and pose problems that they consider important. From Sylvia Ashton Warner to AAUW teacher awardee Judy Logan, good teachers have always known this and have reflected it in their teaching.[33] The schools must find ways to facilitate these processes.

When this is done, issues that may not always be considered "appropriate" will undoubtedly arise. They should. Child abuse is a brutal fact of too many young lives. Children must have a "safe place" to acknowledge their pain and vulnerability and receive help and support. While girls and boys are more or less equally subjected to most forms of physical and emotional abuse, girls confront sexual abuse at four times the rate of boys.

"**P**ublic schools posit separate spheres, that is, they presume that what goes on in school— the public—should be separated from what goes on out of school—the private. Issues that young women experience as private and personal—even if they affect large numbers of adolescents across social classes and racial and ethnic groups—are reserved for discussion inside counselors' offices rather than in classrooms. That domestic violence was a secret not to be discussed in social studies, English, or science, but only in the protected offices of a school psychologist or guidance counselor marks a betrayal of these young women's lives."

M. Fine and N. Zane,
"Bein' Wrapped Too Tight:
When Low-Income Women
Drop Out of High School,"
Women's Studies Quarterly
19 (Spring/Summer
1991):85.

We need to help all children, particularly girls, to know and believe that their bodies are their own to control and use as they feel appropriate—and not objects to be appropriated by others.[34] This, of course, is particularly difficult in a culture that uses the female body to advertise everything from toilet cleanser to truck tires and where the approved female roles remain service-oriented. The so-called "womanly" values of caring for and connecting with others are not ones that women wish to lose, but they are values that must be buttressed by a sense of self and a faith in one's own competence.

In July 1991, *Newsweek* ran a story titled "Girls Who Go Too Far," about the newly aggressive pursuit of boyfriends by some young teens.[35] The comments of the girls themselves illustrate their dilemma in having grown up to believe that a man is an essential part of every woman's life, that only male attention can give them a sense of themselves, and that the culturally accepted way to achieve a goal is to resort to aggressive, even violent, behavior.

Rather than highlighting aggressive behavior among girls, we must address the degree to which violence against women is an increasingly accepted aspect of our culture. School curricula must help girls to understand the extent to which their lives are constrained by fear of rape, the possibility of battering, and the availability of pornography. Boys must be helped to understand that violence damages both the victim and the perpetrator, and that violence against women is not in a somehow-more-acceptable category than other violent acts. The energies and passions so routinely expressed in violence toward others in our culture must be rechanneled and redirected if our society is to fulfill its promise.

A strong line of feminist research and thinking, including the work of Jane Roland Martin, Jean Baker Miller, Carol Gilligan, Nel Noddings, and Mary Belenky and her colleagues, addresses the strengths girls and women can bring to communities through the sense of connection with and concern for others that is more often encouraged and "permitted" in their lives than it is in boys'.[36] Others, such as Alfie Kohn, have written extensively about the need for schools that can help students learn and grow as part of a "prosocial" community.[37] A democracy cannot survive without citizens capable of seeing beyond immediate self-interest to the needs of the larger group.

When asked to describe their ideal school, one group of young women responded:

> *"School would be fun. Our teachers would be excited and lively, not bored. They would act caring and take time to understand how students feel....Boys would treat us with respect....If they run by and grab your tits, they would get into trouble."*[38]

Care, concern, and respect—simple things, but obviously not the norm in many of our nation's classrooms. These young women are not naive. Their full statement recognizes the need to pay teachers well and includes a commitment to "learn by listening and consuming everything" as well as a discussion of parental roles.[39] What they envision is needed by their male classmates and their teachers as well; it is what we as a nation must provide.

"It's important to have a guy so I can feel loved. It doesn't matter if he's ugly or disgusting as long as he pays attention to me."

Junior high student, age fourteen, "Girls Who Go Too Far," *Newsweek*, July 22, 1991.

Gender and Power

Data presented earlier in this report reveal the extent to which girls and boys are treated differently in school classrooms and corridors. These data themselves should be a topic of discussion. They indicate power differentials that are perhaps the most evaded of all topics in our schools. Students are all too aware of "gender politics." In a recent survey, students in Michigan were asked, "Are there any policies, practices, including the behavior of teachers in classrooms, that have the effect of treating students differently based on their sex?" One hundred percent of the middle school and 82 percent of the high school students responding said "yes."[40]

Gender politics is a subject that many in our schools may prefer to ignore, but if we do not begin to discuss more openly the ways in which ascribed power, whether on the basis of race, sex, class, sexual orientation, or religion, affects individual lives, we will not be truly preparing our students for citizenship in a democracy.

PART

THE CHALLENGE:
ACTION
FOR CHANGE

The research reviewed in this report challenges traditional assumptions about the egalitarian nature of American schools. Young women in the United States today are still not participating equally in our educational system. Research documents that girls do not receive equitable amounts of teacher attention, that they are less apt than boys to see themselves reflected in the materials they study, and that they often are not expected or encouraged to pursue higher-level mathematics and science courses. The implications are clear; the system must change.

We now have a window of opportunity that must not be missed. Efforts to improve public education are under way around the nation. We must move girls from the sidelines to the center of educational planning. The nation can no longer afford to ignore the potential of girls and young women. Whether one looks at the issues from an economic, political, or social perspective, girls are one-half of our future.

Significant improvements in the educational opportunities available to girls have occurred in the past two decades. However, twenty years after the passage of Title IX, the achievement of sex- and gender-equitable education remains an elusive dream. The time to turn dreams to reality is now. The current education-reform movement cannot succeed if it continues to ignore half of its constituents. The issues are urgent; our actions must be swift and effective.

Research shows that policies developed to foster the equitable treatment of students and the creation of gender-equitable educational environments can make a difference. They can make a difference, that is, if they are strongly worded and vigorously enforced.

V. Lee, H. Marks, and T. Knowles, "Sexism in Single-Sex and Coeducational Secondary School Classrooms," paper presented at the American Sociological Association annual meeting, Cincinnati, OH, August 1991; S. Bailey and R. Smith, *Policies for the Future*, Council of Chief State School Officers, Washington, DC, 1982.

STRENGTHENED REINFORCEMENT OF TITLE IX IS ESSENTIAL.

1. Require school districts to assess and report on a regular basis to the Office for Civil Rights in the U.S. Department of Education on their own Title IX compliance measures.

2. Fund the Office for Civil Rights at a level that permits increased compliance reviews and full and prompt investigation of Title IX complaints.

3. In assessing the status of Title IX compliance, school districts must include a review of the treatment of pregnant teens and teen parents. Evidence indicates that these students are still the victims of discriminatory treatment in many schools.

TEACHERS, ADMINISTRATORS, AND COUNSELORS MUST BE PREPARED AND ENCOURAGED TO BRING GENDER EQUITY AND AWARENESS TO EVERY ASPECT OF SCHOOLING.

4. State certification standards for teachers and administrators should require course work on gender issues, including new research on women, bias in classroom-interaction patterns, and the ways in which schools can develop and implement gender-fair multicultural curricula.

5. If a national teacher examination is developed, it should include items on methods for achieving gender equity in the classroom and in curricula.

6. Teachers, administrators, and counselors should be evaluated on the degree to which they promote and encourage gender-equitable and multicultural education.

7. Support and released time must be provided by school districts for teacher-initiated research on curricula and classroom variables that affect student learning. Gender equity should be a focus of this research and a criterion for awarding funds.

8. School-improvement efforts must include a focus on the ongoing professional development of teachers and administrators, including those working in specialized areas such as bilingual, compensatory, special, and vocational education.

9. Teacher-training courses must not perpetuate assumptions about the superiority of traits and activities traditionally ascribed to males in our society. Assertive and affiliative skills as well as verbal and mathematical skills must be fostered in both girls, and boys.

10. Teachers must help girls develop positive views of themselves and their futures, as well as an understanding of the obstacles women must overcome in a society where their options and opportunities are still limited by gender stereotypes and assumptions.

THE FORMAL SCHOOL CURRICULUM MUST INCLUDE THE EXPERIENCES OF WOMEN AND MEN FROM ALL WALKS OF LIFE. GIRLS AND BOYS MUST SEE WOMEN AND GIRLS REFLECTED AND VALUED IN THE MATERIALS THEY STUDY.

11. Federal and state funding must be used to support research, development, and follow-up study of gender-fair multicultural curricular models.

12. The Women's Educational Equity Act Program (WEEAP) in the U.S. Department of Education must receive increased funding in order to continue the devel-

opment of curricular materials and models, and to assist school districts in Title IX compliance.

13. School curricula should deal directly with issues of power, gender politics, and violence against women. Better-informed girls are better equipped to make decisions about their futures. Girls and young women who have a strong sense of themselves are better able to confront violence and abuse in their lives.

14. Educational organizations must support, via conferences, meetings, budget deliberations, and policy decisions, the development of gender-fair multicultural curricula in all areas of instruction.

15. Curricula for young children must not perpetuate gender stereotypes and should reflect sensitivity to different learning styles.

GIRLS MUST BE EDUCATED AND ENCOURAGED TO UNDERSTAND THAT MATHEMATICS AND THE SCIENCES ARE IMPORTANT AND RELEVANT TO THEIR LIVES. GIRLS MUST BE ACTIVELY SUPPORTED IN PURSUING EDUCATION AND EMPLOYMENT IN THESE AREAS.

16. Existing equity guidelines should be effectively implemented in all programs supported by local, state, and federal governments. Specific attention must be directed toward including women on planning committees and focusing on girls and women in the goals, instructional strategies, teacher training, and research components of these programs.

17. The federal government must fund and encourage research on the effect on girls and boys of new curricula in the sciences and mathematics. Research is needed particularly in science areas where boys appear to

be improving their performance while girls are not.

18. Educational institutions, professional organizations, and the business community must work together to dispel myths about math and science as "inappropriate" fields for women.

19. Local schools and communities must encourage and support girls studying science and mathematics by showcasing women role models in scientific and technological fields, disseminating career information, and offering "hands-on" experiences and work groups in science and math classes.

20. Local schools should seek strong links with youth-serving organizations that have developed successful out-of-school programs for girls in mathematics and science and with those girls' schools that have developed effective programs in these areas.

CONTINUED ATTENTION TO GENDER EQUITY IN VOCATIONAL EDUCATION PROGRAMS MUST BE A HIGH PRIORITY AT EVERY LEVEL OF EDUCATIONAL GOVERNANCE AND ADMINISTRATION.

21. Linkages must be developed with the private sector to help ensure that girls with training in nontraditional areas find appropriate employment.

22. The use of a discretionary process for awarding vocational-education funds should be encouraged to prompt innovative efforts.

23. All states should be required to make support services (such as child care and transportation) available to both vocational and prevocational students.

24. There must be continuing research on the effectiveness of vocational education for girls and the extent to which the 1990 Vocational Education Amendments benefit girls.

TESTING AND ASSESSMENT MUST SERVE AS STEPPING STONES NOT STOP SIGNS. NEW TESTS AND TESTING TECHNIQUES MUST ACCURATELY REFLECT THE ABILITIES OF BOTH GIRLS AND BOYS.

25. Test scores should not be the only factor considered in admissions or the awarding of scholarships.

26. General aptitude and achievement tests should balance sex differences in item types and contexts. Tests should favor neither females nor males.

27. Tests that relate to "real life situations" should reflect the experiences of both girls and boys.

GIRLS AND WOMEN MUST PLAY A CENTRAL ROLE IN EDUCATIONAL REFORM. THE EXPERIENCES, STRENGTHS, AND NEEDS OF GIRLS FROM EVERY RACE AND SOCIAL CLASS MUST BE CONSIDERED IN ORDER TO PROVIDE EXCELLENCE AND EQUITY FOR ALL OUR NATION'S STUDENTS.

28. National, state, and local governing bodies should ensure that women of diverse backgrounds are equitably represented on committees and commissions on educational reform.

29. Receipt of government funding for in-service and professional development programs should be conditioned upon evidence of efforts to increase the number of women in positions in which they are underrepresented. All levels of government have a role to play in increasing the numbers of women, especially women of color, in education-management and policy positions.

30. The U.S. Department of Education's Office of Educational Research and Improvement (OERI) should establish an advisory panel of gender-equity experts to work with OERI to develop a research and dissemination agenda to foster gender-equitable education in the nation's classrooms.

31. Federal and state agencies must collect, analyze, and report data broken down by race/ethnicity, sex, and some measure of socioeconomic status, such as parental income or education. National standards for use by all school districts should be developed so that data are comparable across district and state lines.

32. National standards for computing dropout rates should be developed for use by all school districts.

33. Professional organizations should ensure that women serve on education-focused committees. Organizations should utilize the expertise of their female membership when developing educational initiatives.

34. Local schools must call on the expertise of teachers, a majority of whom are women, in their restructuring efforts.

35. Women teachers must be encouraged and supported to seek administrative positions and elected office, where they can bring the insights gained in the classroom to the formulation of education policies.

A CRITICAL GOAL OF EDUCATION REFORM MUST BE TO ENABLE STUDENTS TO DEAL EFFECTIVELY WITH THE REALITIES OF THEIR LIVES, PARTICULARLY IN AREAS SUCH AS SEXUALITY AND HEALTH.

36. Strong policies against sexual harassment must be developed. All school personnel must take responsibility for enforcing these policies.

37. Federal and state funding should be used to promote partnerships between schools and community groups, including social service agencies, youth-serving organizations, medical facilities, and local businesses. The needs of students, particularly as highlighted by pregnant teens and teen mothers, require a multi-institutional response.

38. Comprehensive school-based health- and sex-education programs must begin in the early grades and continue sequentially through twelfth grade. These courses must address the topics of reproduction and reproductive health, sexual abuse, drug and alcohol use, and general mental and physical health issues. There must be a special focus on the prevention of AIDS.

39. State and local school board policies should enable and encourage young mothers to complete school, without compromising the quality of education these students receive.

40. Child care for the children of teen mothers must be an integral part of all programs designed to encourage young women to pursue or complete educational programs.

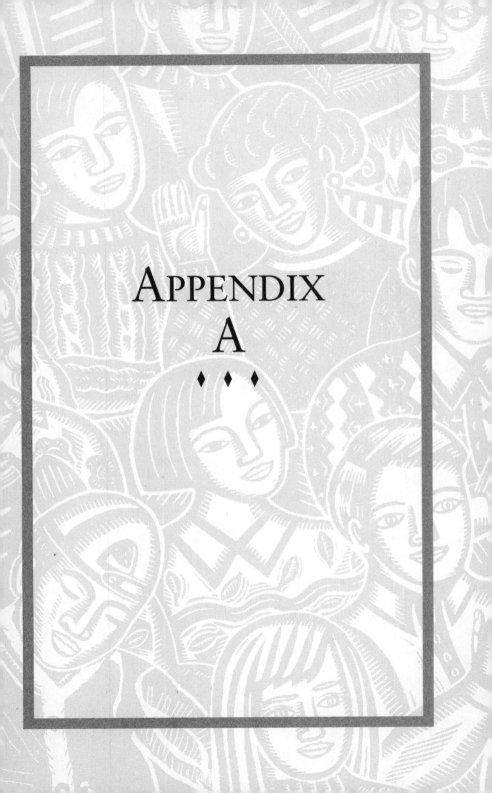

APPENDIX
A

♦ ♦ ♦

Thirty-five Education Reform Reports: Representation of Women on Special Commissions or Task Forces

♦

Report Listed Alphabetically by Title	Year	Sponsor	Total Membership	Number of Women
A Call for Change in Teacher Education	1985	National Commission for Excellence in Teacher Education [American Association of Colleges for Teacher Education]	17	5
A Common Destiny	1989	Committee on the Status of Black Americans [National Research Council]	22	4
A Nation at Risk	1983	National Commission on Excellence in Education [U.S. Dept. of Education]	18	5
A Nation Prepared: Teachers for the 21st Century	1986	Task Force on Teaching as a Profession [Carnegie Forum on Education & Economy]	15	5
Action for Excellence: A Comprehensive Plan to Improve Our Nation's Schools	1983	Task Force on Education for Economic Growth [Education Commission of the States]	43	6
America's Choice: High Skills or Low Wages	1990	Commission on the Skills of the American Work Force [National Center on Education and the Economy]	34	6

Report Listed Alphabetically by Title	Year	Sponsor	Total Membership	Number of Women
America's Shame, America's Hope: Twelve Million Youth at Risk	1989	Advisory Committee [MDC, Inc. for the Mott Foundation]	6	2
Barriers to Excellence: Our Children at Risk	1985	National Board of Inquiry [National Coalition of Advocates for Students]	10	6
Becoming a Nation of Readers	1984	Commission on Reading [National Academy of Education and National Institute of Education]	10	5
Beyond Rhetoric: A New American Agenda for Children and Families	1991	National Commission on Children [set up by Congress: P.L. 100-203]	34	16
Black Initiative and Government Responsibility	1987	Committee on Policy for Racial Justice [Joint Center for Political & Economic Studies]	30	7
Business and Education: Partners for the Future	1985	Advisory Committee [Chamber of Commerce]	8	2
Children in Need: Investment Strategies for the Educationally Disadvantaged	1987	Research and Policy Committee [Committee for Economic Development]	70	2
Educating Americans for the 21st Century	1983	Commission on Precollege Education in Mathematics, Science and Technology [National Science Board]	20	6

Report Listed Alphabetically by Title	Year	Sponsor	Total Membership	Number of Women
Education that Works: An Action Plan for the Education of Minorities	1990	Quality Education for Minorities Project Committee	36	6
Family Support: Education and Involvement: A Guide for State Action	1989	Task Force on Family Education [Council of Chief State School Officers]	8	2
From Gatekeeper to Gateway: Transforming Testing in America	1990	National Commission on Testing and Public Policy	17	3
Hispanic Education: A Statistical Portrait	1990	Advisory Committee for Policy Center [National Council of La Raza]	22	10
Investing in Our Children: Business and the Public Schools	1985	Research and Policy Committee [Committee for Economic Development]	68	2
Leaders for America's Schools	1987	National Commission on Excellence in Educational Administration [University Council for Educational Administration]	26	7
Make Something Happen: Hispanics and Urban School Reform	1984	National Commission on Secondary Schooling for Hispanics [Hispanic Policy Development Project]	16	6

Report Listed Alphabetically by Title	Year	Sponsor	Total Membership	Number of Women
Making the Grade	1983	Task Force on Federal Elementary and Secondary Education Policy [Twentieth Century Fund]	11	3
New Voices: Immigrant Students in U.S. Public Schools	1988	Executive Committee of the National Coalition of Advocates for Students	6	2
One Third of a Nation	1988	Commission on Minority Participation in Education and American Life [American Council on Education and Education Commission of the States]	40	8
Saving the African American Child	1984	Task Force on Academic and Cultural Excellence [National Alliance of Black School Educators]	10	4
Success for All in the New Century	1989	Committee on Educational Equity; Committee on Instruction [Council of Chief State School Officers]	13	4
The Forgotten Half: Non-College Youth in America	1988	Commission on Work, Family and Citizenship [William T. Grant Foundation]	19	4
Three Realities: Minority Life in the United States	1990	Business–Higher Education Forum [American Council on Education]	20	0

Report Listed Alphabetically by Title	Year	Sponsor	Total Membership	Number of Women
Time for Results: The Governors' 1991 Report on Education	1986	Seven Area Task Forces [National Governors' Association]	50	2
Tomorrow's Schools	1990	Project Steering Committee [Holmes Group]	22	7
Tomorrow's Teachers	1986	Executive Committee [Holmes Group]	14	2
Turning Points: Preparing America's Youth for the 21st Century	1989	Task Force on Education of Young Adolescents [Carnegie Foundation]	26	5
Twenty-Two Hispanic Leaders Discuss Poverty	1990	Twenty-Two Leaders [National Council of La Raza]	16	6
Unfinished Agenda: A New Vision for Child Development and Education	1991	Research and Policy Committee [Committee for Economic Development]	57	3
Visions of a Better Way: A Black Appraisal of Public Schooling	1989	Committee on Policy for Racial Justice [Joint Center for Political and EconomicStudies]	30	7

Twenty-two Education Reform Reports:
Research Studies by Single or Multiple Authors

♦

Name of Report/Book	Year	Author(s)	Sponsor or Publisher
A Place Called School	1984	John I. Goodlad	New York: McGraw-Hill Book
An Imperiled Generation: Saving Urban Schools	1988	Gene Maeroff	Carnegie Foundation for the Advancement of Teaching
Changed Lives: Perry Pre-School Program	1984	John Berrueta-Clement et al.	Ypsilanti, MI: High Scope Press
Declining Economic Status of Black Children	1990	Cynthia Rexroat	Washington, D.C.: Joint Center for Political and Economic Studies
Educational Progress: Cities Mobilize to Improve Their Schools	1989	Paul T. Hill, Arthur E. Wise, Leslie Shapiro	Santa Monica, CA: RAND
Framing Dropouts: Notes on the Politics of an Urban Public High School	1991	Michelle Fine	Albany: State University of New York Press
High School	1983	Ernest Boyer	New York: Harper & Row
High School Achievement	1982	James Coleman, Thomas Hoffer, Sally Kilgore	New York: Basic Books
High Schools with Character	1990	Paul T. Hill, Gail Foster, Tamar Gendler	Santa Monica, CA: RAND

Name of Report/Book	Year	Author(s)	Sponsor or Publisher
Horace's Compromise	1984	Theodore Sizer	Boston: Houghton Mifflin
Increasing Achievement of at Risk Students	1990	James McPartland, Robert E. Slavin	U.S. Department of Education
Inside Grade Eight From Apathy to Excitement	1990	John H. Lounsbury, Donald C. Clark	National Association of Secondary School Principals
Longitudinal Study of Structured English Immersion Strategy, Early Exit and Late Exit Transitional Bilingual Education Programs for Language Minority Children	1991	J. David Ramirez, Sandra E. Yuen, Dena R. Ramey	Aguirre International under contract with U.S. Department of Education
Multiplying Inequalities: The Effects of Race, Social Class and Tracking on Opportunities to Learn Mathematics and Science	1990	Jeannie Oakes	RAND for The National Science Foundation
Places Where Teachers Are Taught	1990	John I. Goodlad, Roger Soder, Kenneth A. Sirotnik (Editors)	San Francisco: Jossey-Bass, Initiated by the Center for Educational Renewal of the University of Washington
Public and Private High Schools	1987	James Coleman, Thomas Hoffer	New York: Basic Books
Restructuring America's Schools	1989	Anne Lewis	American Association of School Administrators
Teachers for Our Nation's Schools	1990	John I. Goodlad	San Francisco: Jossey-Bass
The Good High School	1983	Sara Lawrence Lightfoot	New York: Basic Books

Name of Report/Book	Year	Author(s)	Sponsor or Publisher
The Paideia Proposal	1982	Mortimer Adler	Macmillan Publishing Co. for the Paideia Group
Workforce 2000: Work and Workers for the 21st Century	1987	William B. Johnston, Arnold H. Packer	Indianapolis: Hudson Institute
Working in Urban Schools	1989	Thomas Corcoran, Lisa Walker, Lynne White	Washington, D.C.: Institute for Educational Leadership

THE NATIONAL EDUCATION GOALS

♦

Goal 1: Readiness for School

By the year 2000, all children in America will start school ready to learn.

Goal 2: High School Completion

By the year 2000, the high school graduation rate will increase to 90 percent.

Goal 3: Student Achievement and Citizenship

By the year 2000, American students will leave grades 4, 8, and 12 having demonstrated competency in challenging subject matter including English, science, mathematics, history and geography; and every school in America will ensure that all students use their minds well, so they may be prepared for responsible citizenship, further learning, and productive employment in our modern society.

Goal 4: Science and Mathematics

By the year 2000, U.S. students will be first in the world in science and mathematics achievement.

continued...

Goal 5: Adult Literacy and Lifelong Learning

By the year 2000, every adult American will be literate and will possess the knowledge and skills necessary to compete in a global economy and exercise the rights and responsibilities of citizenship.

Goal 6: Safe, Disciplined, and Drug-Free Schools

By the year 2000, every school in America will be free of drugs and violence and will offer a disciplined environment conducive to learning.

*These were the goals that were in place at the time of the original publication of this report, in 1992.

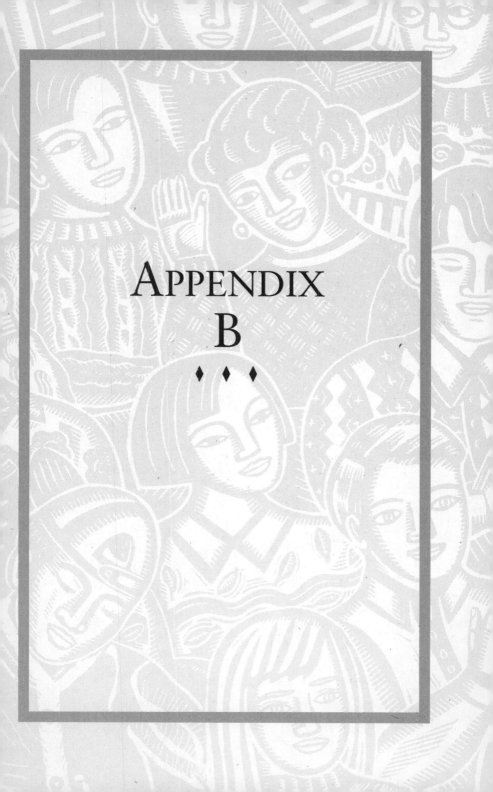

APPENDIX
B

◆ ◆ ◆

THE CONDITION OF INDICATORS ON GENDER EQUITY

♦

Introduction

Research has shown there are differences in how successful students are in school based on their gender and race/ethnicity. Attention has focused on determining the causes of school success and identifying the changes needed to ensure *all* students can succeed to the greatest extent possible.

Recently, there has been a focus on the development and use of education indicators to compare states, school districts, and schools, and to track the progress of reforms. Indicators are statistics derived from tests, surveys, or other data collection activities that describe aspects of the educational system. Indicators typically include descriptions of student backgrounds, school policies and practices, and academic outcomes. They provide information that is useful for policymakers, prac-

titioners, and the public in judging the success of the schools.

Indicators can be analyzed in three ways: as trends over time; as a comparison of groups, programs, or entities responsible for providing services; or with reference to an absolute standard. The indicators described throughout this report reflect these uses or interpretations. Indicator data are collected at the student, teacher, school, district, or state level.

Several indicators related to gender equity in education are important:

♦ How wide are gaps in education achievement and other outcomes between boys and girls?

♦ What levels of education attainment are women reaching, and are they acceptably high?

♦ Do girls and boys have comparable opportunities and do they receive comparable services?

Indicators are most commonly organized around an input-process-output model. The Council of Chief State School Officers (CCSSO) organizes indicators into three areas: (a) **context,** that is, social and economic conditions, such as the context rate of poverty in a community or states; (b) **policies and programs,** which are the processes that can be managed to improve services; and (c) **outcomes,** including academic achievement and other outputs, which are the criteria of accountability or success.

What follows is a discussion of the *condition* of indicators useful for looking at gender equity in education in these three areas.

The Context of Education

In monitoring the quality and *equal*ity of education, many analysts start with the conditions under which schools operate. This is partly to focus attention on the conditions, such as poverty or social problems, that schools must try to overcome. By monitoring the emergence of these conditions, the approach also helps alert the system to students' special needs and helps explain why

outcomes may be different. In general, the validity and availability of these measures are fairly good.

Some background indicators are gender neutral—they describe conditions which affect boys and girls more or less similarly. These include socioeconomic status, majority- or minority-language status, urbanicity of the community, or family conditions, such as nutrition, health care, and parents' marital and domestic status. U.S. Census data[1] provide important information about school populations and about special situations that affect the schools' ability to serve their students.

Data on neonatal conditions, infant deaths, and divorce rates are available at least annually and on a state-by-state basis from the National Center for Health Statistics.[2] Some important statistics in this area are not available, are not collected often enough to be useful, or are not collected at the state or district levels. These include the percentage of children living in poverty, parents' educational attainment, and particularly health and nutritional conditions.

Information on children's preschool experiences is largely nonexistent. Some data on preschool participation and parent-child activities were collected by the National Center for Education Statistics (NCES).[3] The National Education Goals Panel Resource Group on School Readiness recently recommended tracking the preschool conditions of all children, including health care and educational experiences.

Some background indicators are gender-sensitive: conditions that affect girls or women differentially. The most obvious is teen pregnancy. In a probable reflection of traditionally different sex roles in our society, pregnancy and caring for a child are cited more frequently by girls as reasons for dropping out of school. Conversely, violence and criminal involvement are more prevalent among boys, especially poor minority boys. Again, vital health statistics collected through the state-federal system are relatively detailed and comprehensive, showing, for example, on a state-by-state basis the rates at which children are born to young women with varying levels of schooling or the firearm mortality rate for children and youth.[4] Data on peer-

culture conditions are available from surveys conducted for the Department of Health and Human Services. The University of Michigan conducts an annual national survey of a sample of high school seniors to measure rates of alcohol and drug use. The Centers for Disease Control initiated a Youth Risk Behavior Survey in 1990 that will report annually on the health-related behaviors of high school students, including sexual activity, nutrition, smoking, alcohol and drug use, suicide, and violence.

Indicators of School Processes and Services

School processes and services are features of educational programs, under the control of the school system, that affect a student's ability to succeed in school. Some interact with a student's gender, race/ethnicity, and other characteristics. Among the school process indicators most frequently used are program participation, types of course work undertaken by students, and the qualifications of teachers.

One indicator is students' opportunity to learn core curriculum content.

Differences exist in the extent to which boys and girls take courses in science, math, English, history, and other subjects, and in the levels of difficulty, e.g., regular, remedial, honors, or advanced placement, at which they take them. Data are available on courses taken by girls and boys in science and mathematics for sixteen states from the CCSSO Science/Math Indicators Project.[5] NCES collected and reported national course-taking rates by gender and race based on high school transcripts of representative samples of seniors in 1982, 1987, and 1991.[6, 7] Data on actual courses taken would be useful at the school-district level but are unavailable. Course-taking patterns have been related to achievement, education attainment, and career status after high school. These data are available at the national level through two longitudinal studies conducted by NCES.[8, 9] Comparable data are not, however, available for states or school districts.

Participation of students in categorical programs, such as special education, bilingual/English-as-a-second-language programs, and compensatory education, has been found in some research to vary by gender and race/ethnicity. For example, boys are more likely to be identified for certain kinds of special education.[10] Counts of students participating in these programs by gender and racial/ethnic group can serve as indicators of equitable provision of special services as well as selection methods. Data on program participation are reported each year by states to the federal government; however, these data are not always cross-tabulated by racial/ethnic group and gender, and not all data use comparable definitions or collection procedures.

Data on teacher qualifications may reflect the quality of education experiences received by students. Results from the NCES's National Assessment of Education Progress (NAEP) show an association between teacher qualification and student achievement.[11] Teachers' certification status, academic majors, and the courses taken in their education preparation can be used to assess the extent to which girls and boys have equal access to well-qualified teachers. In addition, data on the gender or race/ethnicity of teachers provide an indication of the extent to which girls and minority students have teachers who are role models. Very few data exist on this, even at the national level.

The CCSSO Science/Math Indicators Project has collected and reported state-by-state data on teacher characteristics by gender for forty states.[12] They show the proportion of female teachers in science and math, as well as the qualifications and preparation of science and math teachers in these states. NCES has collected data from national and state-level samples of teachers on teacher certification status, assignments, subject area preparation, age, and experience by gender.[13] Another NCES study, begun in 1988, collects data on the characteristics, preparation, and instructional practices of teachers of a nationally representative cohort of students who will be followed for several years.[14] These data can be used to analyze teacher characteristics and qualifications in relation to students' gender, achievement, and progress beyond high school. National data on teacher characteristics and instructional practices are also collected in a teacher questionnaire as a part of the NAEP.[15] They can be related to student characteristics and achievement in mathematics at the national level (grades 4, 8, and 12) and state level (grade 8) for 1990.

Among the most important effects on girls in school are differential patterns of achievement associated with different classroom experiences. These experiences include subtle but powerful differences in the ways teachers interact with girls compared with boys. Teachers generally interact with and encourage boys more in class, and they send subtle messages concerning their lower expectations of girls in areas such as science and mathematics.[16]

Unfortunately, these more subtle associates of achievement, which would be more valid and useful than cruder measures such as course-taking, are not measured systematically so that we could gauge their extent or monitor whether they are increasing or decreasing. There are no national data on the prevalence of these practices; no states monitor them, and few if any school districts do, although they could be included in teacher-observation procedures. Some data may be available from NCES surveys in this area, based on student perceptions of their interactions with teachers.[17]

Data are available in NCES surveys on student attitudes and expectations in general and toward specific subjects.[18], [19] Boys and girls have shown different attitudes toward the content of academic subjects, their perception of why they do well or poorly, and their perception of the applicability of the content to what they expect to do after high school. These indicators provide valuable information about why girls tend to take or avoid certain courses and why they tend not to go into certain fields of study after high school. Some of them are becoming available state by state through NAEP.

Student Outcomes

Achievement and other outcome data are mixed in their availability by gender. The differences that have been found in available data, however, are substantial. National data from the NAEP are broken down by gender and ethnicity; however, gender-by-ethnicity cross-tabulations are difficult to obtain.[20]

College Board and ACT data are available in detailed breakdowns.[21], [22] Data are provided state by state, but these data are limited in what they can tell us about achievement, because of self-selection, sampling problems, and the different purposes of the tests.

We now have some state-by-state achievement results through NAEP.[23] Eighth-grade math results comparing boys and girls in thirty-seven states indicate different patterns of achievement between genders in general and more specific results when gender is cross-tabulated with race/ethnicity. NAEP achievement results can be examined in relation to background conditions and school programs and processes to get additional insights into achievement differences.

Graduation and other school-completion rates provide further information about the success of various groups of students in high schools. For instance, one can look at the proportions of boys and girls completing a regular high school diploma, an honors diploma, an alternative-program credential, or a credential based on passing the General Education Development

(GED) Tests.[24] While data cross-tabulated by sex and by race/ethnicity provide a better indication of how many students are completing what kinds of programs, very few such data are available. The National Education Goals Panel has requested graduation data by race/ethnicity and by gender. The Office for Civil Rights collects counts of regular diploma recipients by race/ethnicity and gender, but these data are not cross-tabulated.[25]

Data on dropouts are needed to help identify students who are not receiving the educational services or approaches necessary for them to succeed. In order to be most useful, data should be collected by sex, by race/ethnicity, and by grade level when the students drop out. One NCES study is monitoring the dropout rates of a sample of students first identified in the eighth grade.[26] Currently, comparable data are not available for states or school districts; however, in 1991–92 NCES began collecting data from states that are able to provide comparable data using standard procedures.

Information on the reasons why students drop out can focus attention on particular issues affecting students that should be considered in developing special programs. NCES studies will help to determine if boys and girls tend to drop out for different reasons and at different points in their school careers.[27] Many school districts ask students who leave the educational system why they left; however, the reasons stated may not be entirely accurate. Data have been collected on postsecondary education participation patterns of men and women as an indicator of earning power and employment potential. In general, national data collected by NCES show that there are more girls graduating from high school than boys, and that a greater percentage of girls (61 percent) than boys (57 percent) enroll in college after graduating from high school.[28] While more women are awarded bachelor's and master's degrees than men, the pattern is reversed for doctorates and first-professional degrees. Fields of study chosen by men and women also differ. While both men and women tend to major frequently in business and management, education and the health professions are more frequently chosen by women, and engineering is more frequently chosen by men. These findings indicate that women continue to choose as their fields of study majors in which jobs are less well paid. Such data are not available by state.

Conclusions

Despite an abundance of data-collection activities in the United States, there are not enough comparable and useful data on gender differences to adequately monitor the quality and equality of education for boys and girls in the states and the nation. The ways data are collected and maintained at the school, district, and state levels can severely limit the utility of the data.

When data are maintained as part of a comprehensive, automated individual-student record system, the kinds of analyses and cross-tabulations that are needed to answer gender-equity questions are possible. Data maintained in this format allow for more efficient monitoring of the progress of individuals and groups of students (allowing for cross-tabulations of several student variables),

provide the basis for an early-warning system to identify potential problems of students and contribute to the comparability of the data from site to site. This type of system also facilitates the aggregation of data from school to district to state levels.

Renewed interest in gender differences could help bring about changes in the data systems that are required to make policy decisions in this area and to adequately assess improvements to the educational system.

Notes

[1] The National Center for Education Statistics funded the Census Mapping Project, conducted by the Council of Chief State School Officers from 1990-1991. School district boundaries were drawn onto U.S. Census maps. The results will be summary district data from the decennial Census.

[2] Statistics are available in the *Monthly Vital Statistics Report*, published by the National Center for Education Statistics, U.S. Department of Health and Human Services.

[3] The National Center for Education Statistics (NCES) collected data in a National Household Survey in 1991, which was reported in *The National Education Goals Report 1991: Building a Nation of Learners* (Washington, DC: National Goals Panel, 1991).

[4] National Center for Health Statistics, U.S. Department of Health and Human Services, *Monthly Vital Statistics Report*, (Hyattsville, MD: Public Health Service, 1991).

[5] R. Blank and M. Dalkilic, *State Indicators of Science and Mathematics Education 1990* (Washington, DC: Council of Chief State School Officers, 1990).

[6] See, for example, Westat, Inc., *Tabulations for the Nation at Risk Update Study as Part of the 1987 High School Transcript Study* (Washington, DC: U.S. Department of Education, Center for Education Statistics, May 10, 1988).

[7] National Center for Education Statistics, *High School and Beyond: An Analysis of Course-taking Patterns in Secondary Schools as Related to Student Characteristics* (Washington, DC: U.S. Department of Education, 1985).

[8] Ibid.

[9] L. Horn and L. Hafner, *A Profile of American Eighth Grade Mathematics and Science Instruction* (Washington, DC: U.S. Department of Education Office of Educational Research and Improvement, 1990).

[10] Information collected by the Office for Civil Rights, U.S. Department of Education.

[11] I. Mullis et al., *The State of Mathematics Achievement* (Washington, DC: U.S. Department of Education, National Center for Education Statistics, 1991).

[12] Blank and Dalkilic, *State Indicators of Science and Math Education.*

[13] M. McMillen, "Characteristics of Public and Private School Teachers" (Paper presented at the annual meeting of the American Educational Research Association, 1990); and S. A. Bobbitt and M. M. McMillen, "Teacher Training, Certification, and Assignment" (Paper presented at the annual meeting of the American Educational Research Association, 1990).

[14] National Education Longitudinal Study of 1988 (NELS:88) Teacher Questionnaire (Washington, DC: National Center for Education Statistics, U.S. Department of Education, 1988, 1990).

[15] Mullis et al., *The State of Mathematics Achievement.*

[16] D. Sadker and M. Sadker, "Sexism in the Classroom: From Grade School to Grad School," *Phi Delta Kappan* 68 (1986).

[17] Horn and Hafner, *American Eighth Grade Math and Science Instruction.*

[18] Mullis et al., *The State of Mathematics Achievement.*

[19] Horn and Hafner, *American Eighth Grade Math and Science Instruction.*

[20] Mullis et al., *The State of Mathematics Achievement.*

[21] College Entrance Examination Board, *National Report on College-Bound Seniors* (annual reports).

[22] The American College Testing Program, *High School Profile Report* (annual reports).

[23] Mullis et al., *The State of Mathematics Achievement.*

[24] The National Center for Education Statistics collects data about graduates and other completers for each state in the Common Core of Data, but breakouts are not available for different genders within states.

[25] Information collected by the Office for Civil Rights, U.S. Department of Education.

[26] P. Kaufman, M. McMillen, and "S. Whitener, *Dropout Rates in the United States: 1990* (Washington, DC: U.S. Department of Education, National Center for Education Statistics, 1991). The National Education Longitudinal Study (NELS:88) surveyed high school dropouts as part of the 1990 follow-up study. These data will be available in the future.

[27] The 1990 follow-up study of the National Education Longitudinal Study (NELS:88) surveyed high school dropouts. These data will be available in the future.

[28] National Center for Education Statistics, *Digest of Education Statistics 1990* (Washington, DC: U.S. Department of Education, Bureau of Labor Statistics, 1991).

Available Indicators for Monitoring Gender Equity in Education

♦

Indicator	Source	Frequency	Level
Education Context:			
Preschool enrollment	International Association of Educational Assessment	1 time	National
Poverty	U.S. Bureau of the Census	Annual	National
Minority Language Status	U.S. Bureau of the Census	Annual	National
Teen pregnancy	National Center for Health Statistics	Annual	State-by-state
Violence and crime	National Center for Health Statistics	Annual	State-by-state
Drug and alcohol use, high school seniors	Institute for Social Research, University of Michigan	Annual (sample)	National
Health status, grades 9–12	Centers for Disease Control	Annual (sample)	National
School Processes and Services:			
Secondary course taking science/math, grades 7–12	Council of Chief State School Officers	2 years (universe	State-by-state (16 states)
Course taking of high school graduates	National Center for Education Statistics Transcript Study	1982, '87,'91 (sample)	National

Indicator	Source	Frequency	Level
H.S. course taking and careers	National Center for Education Statistics, National Longitudinal Study 72, High School & Beyond, National Education Longitudinal Study 1988	Class of '72, '82, '92 (sample)	National
Special education participation	Office for Civil Rights	Annual (sample) 5 years (universe)	National
Gifted and Talented Program participation	Office for Civil Rights	Annual (sample) 5 years (universe)	National
Compensatory education	U.S. Department of Education, Chapter 1 Office	Annual	State-by-state
Teacher characteristics by teacher gender	Council of Chief State School Officers	2 years	State-by-state, 40 states
Teacher supply and qualifications by teacher gender	National Center for Education Statistics, Schools and Staffing Survey	2 years	State-by-state
Student gender by teacher qualifications and practices by outcomes	National Center for Education Statistics, National Education Longitudinal Survey, 1988	Longitudinal (student sample)	National
Student perceptions of classrooms and student-teacher interactions	National Center for Education Statistics, National Education Longitudinal Survey, 1988	Longitudinal	National

Indicator	Source	Frequency	Level
Student attitudes and expectations, grades 4, 8, 12	National Assessment of Education Progress	2 years by subject (sample)	National, 38 states
Student Outcomes:			
Student achievement, grades 4, 8, 12	National Assessment of Education Progress	2 years by subject (sample)	National, 38 states '90 math
College entrance examination scores	Scholastic Aptitude Test, American College Testing Program	Annual	Voluntary
H.S. graduation/completion	Office for Civil Rights	Annual	National
Dropout rate	National Center for Education Statistics, Common Core of Data	Annual	30 states
College participation/ graduation by field	National Center for Education Statistics, Integrated Postsecondary Education Data System	Annual	National, State-by-state

CONTRIBUTORS

♦ ♦ ♦

Susan M. Bailey is Director of the Wellesley College Center for Research on Women. She has directed the Resource Center on Educational Equity at the Council of Chief State School Officers in Washington, DC, and the Policy Research Office on Women's Education at Harvard and Radcliffe. A former elementary and junior high school teacher, she has a Ph.D. in social science research from the University of Michigan, has conducted postdoctoral research in public health in Latin America, and has lectured and written extensively on issues of gender equity.

Rolf Blank is Director of the Science and Mathematics Indicators Project at the Council of Chief State School Officers, a project that has developed a fifty-state system of indicators and in 1990 produced the first report providing state-by-state data on science and mathematics education in U.S. schools. Formerly, he was a staff member at the National Academy of Science/National Research Council. He holds a Ph.D. in sociology from Florida State University.

Lynn Burbridge is an Associate Director and Research Associate at the Wellesley College Center for Research on Women. She has a Ph.D. in economics from Stanford University; her research has focused on the impact of public policies on minorities, women, and youth. Her previous experience includes research at the Urban Institute and the Joint Center for Political and Economic Studies in Washington, DC.

Patricia B. Campbell is Director of Campbell-Kibler Associates, a research and evaluation consulting firm. Formerly Associate Professor of Research, Measurement and Statistics at Georgia State University, she has degrees in mathematics and instructional technology and a Ph.D. in teacher education from Syracuse University. She has written extensively; her books, book chapters, and articles include "Redefining the 'Girl Problem' in Mathematics" and *What Will Happen If...Young Children and the Scientific Method.*

Barbara S. Clements is Assistant Director of the State Education Assessment Center of the Council of Chief State School Officers. She directs several projects that focus on improving the comparability and comprehensiveness of data collected about public schools. Previously, she was a Program Director at the Texas Education Agency. She received a Ph.D. in education statistics and evaluation from the University of Texas at Austin.

Janice Earle is Program Director for the National Science Foundation's Statewide Systematic Initiative Program. Prior to joining NSF, she directed the Center on Educational Equity at the National Association of State Boards of Education. A former history teacher, her publications include *Female Dropouts: A New Perspective.* She has a Ph.D. in educational policy, planning, and administration from the University of Maryland.

Barbara Jackson is Professor at the Graduate School of Education at Fordham University. She has an Ed.D. from the Graduate School of Education at Harvard University. Formerly, she served as Professor and Dean of the School of Education at Morgan State University and as Associate Professor at Atlanta University. Among her many articles is "Parent Choice and Empowerment: New Roles for Parents," written with Bruce Cooper.

Fern Marx is a Research Associate at the Wellesley College Center for Research on Women, where she directs the Center's Teen Parent Project. She is a mid-career fellow at the Yale University Bush Center in Child Development and Social Policy. She has written widely on child care, early childhood education, and teen pregnancy, and is a doctoral candidate at the Florence Heller School, Brandeis University.

Peggy McIntosh is an Associate Director at the Wellesley College Center for Research on Women and founder and co-director of the K–12 National SEED Project on Inclusive Curriculum (Seeking Educational Equity and Diversity). She has taught at the elementary and secondary school levels and has held several university positions. Her Ph.D. in English is from Harvard University. She writes and lectures on women's studies, curriculum change, and systems of unearned privilege.

David Sadker is Professor at the School of Education at American University in Washington, DC. He has an Ed.D. from the University of Massachusetts and has written more than 75 articles on gender-equity issues. With Myra Sadker he co-authored *The Sex Equity Handbook for Schools*.

Myra Sadker (1943–1995) was Professor at the School of Education at American University. Her Ed.D. is from the University of Massachusetts. In 1973 she wrote the first major book dealing with sex equity in education, *Sexism in School and Society*. Over the past decade she has co-directed grants dealing with equity and effectiveness in classroom interaction. David and Myra Sadker have conducted training on educational-equity issues in more than forty states.

Ramsey Selden is Director of the State Education Assessment Center of the Council of Chief State School Officers. He coordinates the Council's work on educational assessment, indicators, and the improvement of educational statistics. He worked previously at the National Institute of Education and contributed to the work of the National Commission on Excellence in Education. He completed his Ph.D. in educational research at the University of Virginia.

Margaret L. Stubbs is currently a consultant to schools on a variety of topics, including girls' and women's development, sex-equitable sex education, and teacher-initiated research. A classroom teacher with experience at the elementary and junior high/middle school levels, she is now teaching a college-level course on human sexuality. Her Ph.D. in developmental psychology is from Brandeis University. Among her many publications is the series *Body Talk*, designed to facilitate discussion among parents and children.

Gretchen Wilbur is an independent consultant who works with projects related to education, equity, and collaborative management. She received her Ph.D. from Vanderbilt University in educational leadership, with a specialization in program and staff development. Formerly Executive Director of Curriculum for the Kansas City School District, she has managed several projects designed to promote sex- and gender-equity in public education.

ENDNOTES

♦ ♦ ♦

PART ONE

[1] See Appendix A.

[2] The only women in leadership positions on the thirty-five commissions and task forces we reviewed were: Judith Lanier, President of the Holmes Group; Marian Wright Edelman, Cochair of the National Coalition of Advocates for Students National Board of Inquiry; Eleanor Holmes Norton, Cochair of the Joint Center for Political and Economic Studies' Committee on Policy for Racial Justice; Cecily Cannon Selby, Cochair of the National Science Board's Commission on Precollege Education and Mathematics, Science and Technology; Mari-Luci Jaramillo, Cochair of the Hispanic Policy Development Project; and Barbara Sizemore, Cochair of the National Alliance of Black School Educators' Task Force on Academic and Cultural Excellence. Eleanor Farrar was Staff Coordinator for the report *Black Initiative and Government Responsibility*; Cheryl Hayes was Executive Director of the National Commission on Children; Shirley McBay directed the development of *Education That Works*, and Glenda Partee was the principal author for *Family Support, Education and Involvement*.

[3] The only one of the thirty-five reports without women on the oversight group was *Three Realities: Minority Life in the United States*, sponsored by the Business–Higher Education forum in affiliation with the American Council of Education. See Appendix A for further information.

[4] The four reports were: *A Common Destiny; Barriers to Excellence: Our Children at Risk; From Gatekeeper to Gateway: Transforming Testing in America; Turning Points: Preparing America's Youth for the 21st Century.*

[5] National Coalition of Advocates for Students, *Barriers to Excellence: Our Children at Risk* (New York: National Board of Inquiry, 1985), p. 21.

[6] Ibid., p. 104.

[7] R. Schmuck and P. Schmuck, *Small Districts, Big Problems: Making Schools Everybody's House* (Newbury Park, CA: Corwin Press, 1992).

[8] National Governors Association, *National Educational Goals* (Washington, DC: 1990). See Appendix A for a list of the goals.

[9] *America 2000: An Education Strategy* (Washington, DC: U.S. Department of Education, 1991), p. 1.

[10] *Education for All: Women and Girls Speak Out on the National Education Goals* (Washington, DC: National Coalition for Women and Girls in Education, 1990); see also testimony submitted to the National Education Goals Panel by the National Coalition for Women and Girls in Education, May 1991.

[11] S. Thompson, "Gender Labels and Early Sex Role Development," *Child Development of Sex Role Stereotypes in the Third Year* 46 (1975):339–47; M. Weinraub et al., "The Third Year: Relationships to Gender Labeling, Gender Identity, Sex-Typed Toy Preference, and Family Characteristics," *Child Development* 55 (1984):1493–1503; G. Cowan and C. Hoffman, "Gender Stereotyping in Young Children: Evidence to Support a Concept-Learning Approach," *Sex Roles* 14 (1986):211–24.

[12] C. Edwards and P. Ramsey, *Promoting Social and Moral Development in Young Children: Creative Approaches for the Classroom* (New York: Teachers College Press, 1986), p. 67; J. Roopnarine, "Sex-Typed Socialization in Mixed-Age Preschool Classrooms," *Child Development* 55 (1984):1078–84; N. Eisenberg, K. Tryon, and E. Cameron, "The Relation of

Preschoolers' Peer Interaction to Their Sex-Typed Toy Choices," *Child Development* 55 (1984):1044–50; C. Martin and J. Little, "The Relation of Gender Understanding to Children's Sex-Typed Preferences and Gender Stereotypes," *Child Development* 61 (1990):1427–39; J. Smetana, "Preschool Children's Conceptions of Sex-Role Transgressions," *Child Development* 57 (1986):862–71; Cowan and Hoffman, "Gender Stereotyping."

13 Edwards and Ramsey, *Promoting Social and Moral Development;* J. Blomberg, "Sex-Typed Channeling Behavior in the Preschool Peer Group: A Study of Toy Choice in Same Sex and Cross Sex Play Dyads" (Ph.D. diss. University of California at Berkeley, 1981); M. O'Brien and A. Huston, "Development of Sex-Typed Play Behavior in Toddlers," *Developmental Psychology* 21 (1985):866–71; D. Perry, A. White, and L. Perry, "Does Early Sex Typing Result from Children's Attempts to Match Their Behavior to Sex Role Stereotypes?" *Child Development* 55 (1984):2114–21.

14 D. Perry and K. Bussey, *Social Development* (Englewood Cliffs, NJ: Prentice Hall, 1984) as cited in M. Cole and S. Cole, *The Development of Children* (New York: Scientific American Books, 1989) p. 353; A. Cann and S. Newbern, "Sex Stereotype Effects in Children's Picture Recognition," *Child Development* 55 (1984):1085–90; W. Emmerich and K. Shepard, "Cognitive Factors in the Development of Sex-Typed Preferences," *Sex Roles* 11 (1984):997–1007.

15 E. Maccoby and C. Jacklin, "Gender Segregation in Childhood," in *Advances in Child Development and Behavior,* H. Reese, ed. (New York: Academic Press, 1987), 20:239–88; Edwards and Ramsey, *Promoting Social and Moral Development;* L. Hayden-Thomson, K. Rubin, and S. Hymel, "Sex Preferences in Sociometric Choices," *Developmental Psychology* 23 (1987):558–62.

16 Edwards and Ramsey, *Promoting Social and Moral Development;* L. Serbin and C. Sprafkin, "The Salience of Gender and the

Process of Sex Typing in Three- to Seven-Year-Old Children," *Child Development* 57 (1986):1188–99.

17 B. Thorne, "Girls and Boys Together... But Mostly Apart: Gender Arrangements in Elementary Schools," in *Relationships and Development,* W. Hartup and Z. Rubin, eds. (Hillsdale, NJ: Lawrence Erlbaum Associates, 1986), pp.167–84; R. Best, *We've All Got Scars: What Boys and Girls Learn in Elementary School* (Bloomington, IN: Indiana University Press, 1983); see also B. Kerr, *Smart Girls, Gifted Women* (Columbus, OH: Psychology Publishing Co., 1985).

18 S. Nolen-Hoeksema, J. Girgus, and M. Seligman, "Sex Differences in Depression and Explanatory Style in Children," *Journal of Youth and Adolescence* 20 (April 1991):241.

19 M. Rutter, "The Developmental Psychopathology of Depression: Issues and Perspectives," in *Depression in Young People: Developmental and Clinical Perspectives,* M. Rutter, C. Izard, and P. Read, eds. (New York: The Guilford Press, 1986), p. 13; C. Izard and G. Schwartz, "Patterns of Emotion in Depression," in *Depression in Young People.*

20 L. Brown in her paper "A Problem of Vision: The Development of Voice and Relational Knowledge in Girls Ages 7–16," *Women's Studies Quarterly* 19 (Spring/Summer 1991):52–72, writes of the clarity and strength of young girls and their ability to maintain authenticity in relationships.

21 R. Simmons and D. Blyth, *Moving into Adolescence: The Impact of Pubertal Change and the School Context* (New York: Aldine de Gruyter Press, 1987), p. 125.

22 J. Brooks-Gunn and A. Petersen, *Girls at Puberty* (New York: Plenum Press, 1983), p. 110.

23 Ibid., p.113.

24 D. Bush and R. Simmons, "Gender and Coping with the Entry into Early Adolescence," in *Gender and Stress,* R. Barnett, L. Biener, and G. Baruch, eds. (New York: Free Press, 1987), pp. 185–211.

[25] J. Brooks-Gunn and M. Warren, "Measuring Physical Status and Timing in Early Adolescence: A Developmental Perspective," *Journal of Youth and Adolescence* 14 (1985):163–89; J. Rierdan, E. Koff, and M. Stubbs, "Gender, Depression and Body Image in Early Adolescents," *Journal of Early Adolescence* 8 (1988): 109–17.

[26] Simmons and Blyth, *Moving into Adolescence*, p. 72.

[27] D. Buhrmester and W. Ferman, "The Development of Companionship and Intimacy," *Child Development* 58 (1987):1101–13.

[28] Simmons and Blyth, *Moving into Adolescence*, p. 72.

[29] *Shortchanging Girls, Shortchanging America: A Call to Action* (Washington, DC: American Association of University Women, 1991), p. 10; Simmons and Blyth, *Moving into Adolescence*; S. Harter, "Self and Identity Development," in *At the Threshold: The Developing Adolescent*, S. Feldman and G. Elliott, eds. (Cambridge, MA: Harvard University Press, 1990), pp. 352–89; C. Gilligan, N. Lyons, and T. Hammer, eds., *Making Connections: The Relational Worlds of Adolescent Girls at Emma Willard School* (Cambridge, MA: Harvard University Press, 1990).

[30] *Shortchanging Girls*, p. 10.

[31] Unpublished data from the American Association of University Women 1990 Poll (Washington, DC: Greenberg-Lake: The Analysis Group).

[32] Simmons and Blyth, *Moving into Adolescence*, p. 227.

[33] A. Peterson, P. Sarigiani, and R. Kennedy, "Adolescent Depression: Why More Girls?" *Journal of Youth and Adolescence* 20 (April 1991):247–71.

[34] Bush and Simmons, "Gender and Coping," p. 208.

PART TWO

....

[1] U.S. Department of Education, Office of Educational Research and Improvement, National Center for Education Statistics, *Digest of Education Statistics*, 1990, NCES 91-660, pp. 43, 61.

[2] S. Greenberg, "Educational Equity in Early Education Environments," in *Handbook for Achieving Sex Equity through Education*, S. Klein, ed. (Baltimore, MD: Johns Hopkins University Press, 1985), p. 457.

[3] G. Ranck, "Are We Shortchanging Girls? A Response to 'Are We Shortchanging Boys?'" *Child Care Information Exchange* (July–August 1991):20–22.

[4] Greenberg, "Educational Equity," p. 460; A. Pellegrini and J. Perlmutter, "Classroom Contextual Effects on Children's Play," *Developmental Psychology* 25 (1989): 289–96.

[5] J. Larsen and C. Robinson, "Later Effects of Preschool on Low-Risk Children," *Early Childhood Research Quarterly* 4 (1989):133–44.

[6] See for example, L. Schweinhart, D. Weikart, and M. Larner, "Consequences of Three Preschool Curriculum Models Through Age 15," *Early Childhood Research Quarterly* 1 (1986):15–45.

[7] L. Miller and R. Bizzell, "Long-Term Effects of Four Preschool Programs: Ninth

and Tenth Grade Results," *Child Development* 55 (1984):1570–87.

[8] See for example, D. Rock et al., *Study of Excellence in High School: Longitudinal Study* (Princeton, NJ: Educational Testing Service, 1986).

[9] This survey of the current literature on girls' achievement is based on original research with a major exception. Results of a method called meta-analysis were used to explore gender differences in performance. Meta-analysis is the application of quantitative methods to combine evidence from different studies. In meta-analysis the effect size d is computed; d is the difference between the female mean score and the male mean score divided by the pooled within-group standard deviation. Because it looks at the relative size of gender differences, meta-analysis is considered a more valid way of summarizing the literature in a specific area than, for example, counting the studies that find gender differences and those that do not. When interpreting meta-analysis results, it is important to remember that effect sizes of .2 or less are considered small, while those close to .5 are considered of medium size, and effect sizes of .8 and higher are considered large.

[10] E. Maccoby and C. Jacklin, *The Psychology of Sex Differences* (Stanford, CA: Stanford University Press, 1974), p. 84.

[11] Ibid.; D. Denno, "Sex Differences in Cognition: A Review and Critique of the Longitudinal Evidence," *Adolescence* 17 (Winter 1982):779–88.

[12] J. Hyde and M. Linn, "Gender Differences in Verbal Activity: A Meta-Analysis," *Psychological Bulletin* 104 (January 1988):53–69.

[13] D. Halpern, "The Disappearance of Cognitive Gender Differences: What You See Depends on Where You Look," *American Psychologist* 44 (August 1989):1156–57.

[14] Hyde and Linn, "Gender Differences," p. 63. See Appendix B for a more thorough discussion of this issue.

[15] I. Mullis and L. Jenkins, *The Reading Report Card, 1971–88: Trends from the Nation's Report Card* (Princeton, NJ: Educational Testing Service, 1990); I. Mullis, E. Owens, and G. Phillips, *Accelerating Academic Achievement: A Summary of Findings from 20 Years of NAEP* (Washington, DC: U.S. Department of Education, 1990).

[16] U.S. Department of Education, National Center for Education Statistics, *The Tested Achievement of the National Education Longitudinal Study of 1988 Eighth Grade Class,* December 1990.

[17] M. Hogrebe, S. Nist, and I. Newman, "Are There Gender Differences in Reading Achievement? An Investigation Using the High School and Beyond Data," *Journal of Educational Psychology* 77 (1985):716–24; Rock et al., *Study of Excellence in High School Education: Longitudinal Study, 1980–82 Final Report* (Washington, DC: U.S. Department of Education Center for Statistics, 1986); L. Winfield and V. Lee, "Gender Differences in Reading Proficiency: Are They Constant Across Racial Groups?" presented at the Annual Meeting of the American Psychological Association, Washington, DC, August 26, 1986.

[18] See Winfield and Lee, "Gender Differences in Reading Proficiency."

[19] National Assessment of Education Progress, *Reading Comprehension of American Youth: Do They Understand What They Read?* (Princeton, NJ: Educational Testing Service, 1982).

[20] Mullis, Owens, and Phillips, *Accelerating Academic Achievement.*

[21] National Assessment of Educational Progress, *Reading Comprehension of American Youth.*

[22] Hogrebe, Nist, and Newman, "Are There Gender Differences in Reading?" p. 721.

[23] Ibid.; B. Hare, *Black Girls: A Comparative Analysis of Self-Perception and Achievement by Race, Sex, and Socioeconomic Background* (Baltimore, MD: The Johns Hopkins University Center for Social Organization of Schools, 1979).

[24] Mullis, Owens, and Phillips, "Accelerating Academic Achievement," p. 52.

[25] B. Arbrorough and R. Johnson, "Sex Differences in Written Language Among Elementary Pupils: A Seven Year Longitudinal Study," *Psychological Reports* 64 (1989):407–14.

[26] A second caution concerns using the Scholastic Aptitude Test results as a measure of gender differences in math. While the sheer number of students taking the SAT makes it an attractive and frequently used basis of comparison, the gender differences that are found using the SAT are much larger than those found on comparable tests.

[27] L. Friedman, "Mathematics and the Gender Gap: A Meta-Analysis of Recent Studies on Sex Differences in Mathematical Tasks," *Review of Educational Research* 59 (1989):185–213; J. Hyde, E. Fennema, and S. Lamon, "Gender Differences in Mathematics Performance: A Meta-Analysis," *Psychological Bulletin* 107 (1990):139–55.

[28] G. Wilder and K. Powell, *Sex Differences in Test Performance: A Survey of the Literature*, College Board Report 8903, ETS RR 89-4, (New York: College Board Publications, [1989]); A. Kolstad and J. Thorne, "Changes in High School Course Work from 1982 to 1987: Evidence from Two National Surveys," paper presented at the annual meeting of the American Educational Research Association, San Francisco, March 1989.

[29] Hyde, Fennema, and Lamon, "Gender Differences."

[30] Ibid.

[31] J. Dossey et al., *The Mathematics Report Card*, 17-M-01 (Princeton, NJ: Educational Testing Service, 1988), pp. 54–55; *Women and Minorities in Science and Engineering* (Washington, DC: National Science Foundation, 1990), p. 14.

[32] I. Mullis et al., *The State of Mathematics Achievement: NAEP's 1990 Assessment of the Nation and the Trial Assessment of the States* (Princeton, NJ: Educational Testing Service, 1991), p. 15.

[33] Dossey et al., *The Mathematics Report Card*, pp. 54–55; "The Gender Gap in Education: How Early and How Large," *Educational Testing Service Policy Notes* 2 (October 1989).

[34] *1988 Profiles of SAT and Achievement Test Takers* (Princeton NJ: Educational Testing Service, 1988); *Women and Minorities.*

[35] J. Stockard and J. Wood, "The Myth of Female Underachievement: A Reexamination of Sex Differences in Academic Underachievement," *American Education Research Journal* 21 (1984):825–38; T. Dick and S. Rallis, "Factors and Influences on High School Students' Career Choices," *Journal of Research in Mathematics Education,* 22 (1991):281–292.

[36] *Women and Minorities*, p. 15.

[37] Friedman, "Mathematics and the Gender Gap."

[38] P. Brandon, B. Newton, and O. Hammond, "Children's Mathematics Achievement in Hawaii: Sex Differences Favoring Girls," *American Educational Research Journal* 24 (1987):25–36.

[39] Friedman, "Mathematics and the Gender Gap"; Hyde, Fennema, and Lamon, "Gender Differences"; E. Moore and A. Smith, "Sex and Ethnic Groups Differences in Mathematics Achievement: Results from the National Longitudinal Study," *Journal for Research in Mathematics Education* 18 (1987):25–36.

[40] M. Linn and J. Hyde, "Gender, Mathematics and Science," *Educational Researcher* 18 (November 1989):17–27.

[41] A. Lapointe, N. Mead, and G. Phillips, *World of Difference: An International Assessment of Mathematics and Science* (Princeton, NJ: Educational Testing Service, 1989).

[42] Mullis et al., *The State of Mathematics Achievement*, p. 6.

[43] I. Mullis and L. Jenkins, *The Science Report Card*, report No. 17-S-01 (Princeton, NJ: Educational Testing Service, [1988]), pp. 30–31; Lapointe,

Mead, and Phillips, *World of Difference.*

[44] Mullis and Jenkins, *The Science Report Card,* pp. 107–13; *Women and Minorities,* p. 14.

[45] Mullis and Jenkins, *The Science Report Card.*

[46] Stockard and Wood, "The Myth"; S. Rallis and R. Ahern, "Math and Science Education in High Schools: A Question of Sex Equity," paper presented at the annual meeting of the American Educational Research Association, San Francisco, April 1986; Dick and Rallis, "Factors and Influences."

[47] Lapointe, Mead, and Phillips, *World of Difference.*

[48] National Science Board, *Science and Engineering Indicators–1989* (Washington, DC: National Science Foundation, 1990).

[49] Mullis et al., *The State of Mathematics Achievement,* p. 32.

[50] R. Blank and M. Dalkilis, *State Indicators of Science and Mathematics Education, 1990* (Washington, DC: Council of Chief State Officers, State Education Assessment Center, 1991).

[51] National Science Board, *Indicators–1989.*

[52] Kolstad and Thorne, "Changes in High School Course Work."

[53] National Science Board, *Indicators–1989; Women and Minorities,* p. 15.

[54] National Science Board, *Indicators–1989.*

[55] Blank and Dalkilis, *State Indicators of Science and Mathematics Education,* 1990.

[56] Mullis et al., *Women and Minorities,* p. 30.

[57] Dick and Rallis, "Factors and Influences."

[58] N. Hewitt and E. Seymour, "Factors Contributing to High Attrition Rates Among Science and Engineering Undergraduate Majors," report to the Alfred P. Sloan Foundation, [26 April 1991], p. 100.

[59] P. Campbell and S. Metz, "What Does It Take to Increase the Number of Women Majoring in Engineering?" conference proceedings of the American Society for Engineering Education, 1987, pp. 882–87.

[60] J. Kahle and M. Lakes, "The Myth of Equality in Science Classrooms," *Journal of Research in Science Teaching* 20 (1983): 131–40.

[61] Mullis and Jenkins, *The Science Report Card,* pp. 30–33.

[62] L. Zimmer and S. Bennett, "Gender Differences on the California Statewide Assessment of Attitudes and Achievement in Science," paper presented at the annual meeting of the American Educational Research Association, Washington, DC, 1987. Unlike Mullis and Jenkins, authors of *The Science Report Card,* Zimmer and Bennett found girls using microscopes in numbers equal to boys.

[63] Ibid.

[64] L. Reyes and G. Stanic, "Race, Sex and Math," *Journal of Research in Math Education* 19 (1988):26–43.

[65] E. Fennema and J. Sherman, "Sex Related Differences in Math Achievement, Spatial Visualization and Affective Factors," *American Educational Research Journal* 14 (1977):51–71; L. Reyes, "Affective Variables and Mathematics Education," *The Elementary School Journal* 84 (1984):558–81.

[66] Reyes, "Affective Variables."

[67] Dossey et al., *The Mathematics Report Card,* 17-M-01 (Princeton, NJ: Educational Testing Service, 1988).

[68] Fennema and Sherman, "Sex Related Differences."

[69] A. Kelly, "Does That Train Set Matter? Scientific Hobbies and Science Achievement and Choice," paper presented at the Girls and Technology Conference, Ann Arbor, July 1987; J. Eccles, "Bringing Young Women to Math and Science," in *Gender and Thought: Psychological Perspectives,* M. Crawford and M. Gentry, eds. (New York: Springer-Verlag, 1989), pp. 36–58.

[70] C. Leder, "Teacher/Student Interactions in the Mathematics Classroom: A Different Perspective," in *Mathematics and Gender: Influences on Teachers and Students*, E. Fennema and C. Leder, eds. (New York: Teachers College, 1990), pp. 149–68.

[71] American Association of University Women, *Shortchanging Girls, Shortchanging America* (Washington, DC: American Association of University Women, 1990), p. 13.

[72] Campbell and Metz, "The Number of Women Majoring in Engineering," pp. 882–87.

[73] P. MacCorquodale, "Self-Image Science and Math: Does the Image of 'Scientist' Keep Girls and Minorities from Pursuing Science and Math," paper presented at the American Sociological Association, San Antonio, 1984.

[74] American Association of University Women, *Shortchanging Girls*, p. 14.

[75] Ibid.

[76] J. Armstrong, "A National Assessment of Participation and Achievement of Women in Mathematics," in *Women and Mathematics: Balancing the Equation*, C. Chipman, L. Brush, and D. Wilson, eds.(Hillsdale, NJ: Erlbaum, 1985), pp. 56–94.

[77] Ibid.

[78] Ibid.

[79] Hyde, Fennema, and Lamon, "Gender Differences."

[80] L. Tartre and E. Fennema, "Mathematics Achievement and Gender: A Longitudinal Study of Selected Cognitive and Affective Factors (Grades 6–12)," paper presented at the annual meeting of the American Educational Research Association, Chicago, April 1991.

[81] J. Oakes, *Lost Talent: The Underparticipation of Women, Minorities and Disabled Persons in Science* (Santa Monica, CA: RAND Institute, 1990).

[82] P. Flores, "How Dick and Jane Perform Differently in Geometry: Test Results on Reasoning, Visualization, Transformation, Applications and Coordinates," paper presented at the annual meeting of the American Educational Research Association, Boston, 1990.

[83] J. Kahle, "Why Girls Don't Know," in *What Research Says to the Science Teacher: The Process of Knowing*, vol. 6, M. Rowe, ed. (Washington, DC: National Science Teachers' Association, 1990); P. Campbell, *Eureka! Participant Follow-Up Analysis*, (Groton, MA: Campbell-Kibler Associates, 1990).

[84] A review of the literature identified only one study examining gender differences in bilingual education. It noted the sex-stereotyping found in some of the books used in bilingual courses. M. Spencer and P. Lewis, "Sex Equity in Bilingual Education, English as a Second Language, and Foreign Language Instruction," *Theory into Practice* 25 (Autumn 1986):257–65.

[85] B. Williams, P. Richmond, and B. Mason, *Designs for Compensatory Education: Conference Proceedings and Papers* (Washington, DC: Research and Evaluation Associates, Inc., 1987); Council of Chief State School Officers, *School Success for Limited English Proficient Students* (Washington, DC: Council of Chief State School Officers, 1990). The proceedings from the compensatory-education conference cite the dearth of research by gender, economic status, and culture.

[86] In the NELS, socioeconomic status is a composite variable based on father's education, mother's education, father's occupation, mother's occupation, and family income. In HSB, socioeconomic status is a composite of father's occupation, father's education, mother's education, family income, and material possessions in the household.

[87] For copies of the tables and a more detailed discussion of these tables, see Lynn C. Burbridge, "The Interaction of Race, Gender, and Socioeconomic Status in Education Outcomes," presented at the American Sociological Association Annual Meeting, August 24, 1991.

[88] This has been recognized at least since

the publication of James Coleman's seminal report, *Equality of Educational Opportunity* (Washington, DC: U.S. Department of Health, Education, and Welfare, 1966). Previous research indicated that, when student populations are matched by socioeconomic status, blacks and Hispanics are *less* likely than whites to drop out of school and are more likely to go on to college. See L. Weis, E. Farrar, and H. Petrie, *Dropouts from School: Issues Dilemmas and Solutions* (Albany, NY: State University of New York Press, 1989).

[89] As indicated earlier, girls consistently earn higher grades than boys and are less likely to be held back at year's end, regardless of socioeconomic status. But grading and being held back may reflect perceptions of students' discipline and cooperativeness as well as their knowledge.

[90] A recent analysis of the NELS confirms these findings: At the two-year follow-up, 6.8 percent of the students had dropped out of school before the tenth grade. Dropouts were disproportionately male and minority. See "First National Study of Young Dropouts Finds 6.8% Leave Before 10th Grade," *Education Week*, September 25, 1991.

[91] E. Smith, "The Black Female Adolescent: A Review of the Educational, Career, and Psychological Literature," *Psychology of Women Quarterly* 6 (1982); N. St. John and R. Lewis, "Race and Social Structure of the Elementary School Classroom," *Sociology of Education* 48 (1975):346–68; H. Sagar and J. Schofield, *Classroom Interaction Patterns Among Black and White Boys and Girls* (Washington, DC: National Institute of Education, 1980).

[92] K. Neckerman and W. Wilson, "Schools and Poor Communities," in Council of Chief State School Officers, *School Success for Students at Risk* (Orlando, FL: Harcourt Brace Jovanovich, Inc., 1988), pp. 25–44.

[93] J. Ogbu, *Minority Education and Caste* (New York: Academic Press, 1978).

[94] Data on the Advanced Placement exam for the years 1986 through 1990 were pro-

vided by the Educational Testing Service in Princeton, New Jersey. (The tests are administered by the College Board.) Data reported here are for 1990, but the same patterns are found since 1986, when data by race and gender first became available.

[95] It must be kept in mind, however, that minorities represent a small proportion of all AP test takers: African Americans, Hispanics, and Native Americans represent 27 percent of all students in 1990, but only 10 percent of AP test takers. Asians, on the other hand, represent less than 3 percent of all students, but 13 percent of AP test takers. Whites take the AP exam in proportion to their representation in the school population: 70 percent.

[96] J. Kozol, *Savage Inequalities: Children in America's Schools* (New York: Crown Publishing, 1991).

[97] The National Commission on Children has addressed the financial issues in some detail. See United States National Commission on Children, *Beyond Rhetoric: A New American Agenda for Children and Families: Final Report of the National Commission on Children* (Washington, DC: The National Commission on Children, Superintendent of Documents, U.S. Government Printing Office, 1991).

[98] F. Furstenberg, Jr., "As the Pendulum Swings: Teenage Childbearing and Social Concern," *Family Relations* 40 (1991): 127–38.

[99] A. Geronimus, "Why Teenage Childbearing Might Be Sensible: Research and Policy Implications," paper presented at the annual meeting of the American Association for the Advancement of Science, New Orleans, LA, 1990; A. Geronimus and S. Korenman, "The Socioeconomic Consequences of Teen Childbearing Reconsidered," discussion paper 90-190, Ann Arbor, MI: Population Studies Center, University of Michigan, 1990; K. Luker, "The Social Construction of Teenage Pregnancy," paper presented at the annual meeting of the American Sociological Association, Washington, DC, August 1990. These ref-

erences are cited in Furstenberg, "As the Pendulum Swings."

[100] U.S. Department of Health and Human Services, National Center for Health Statistics, *Vital Statistics of the United States*, 1988, vol. 1, Table 1–67, p. 64; C. Westoff, G. Cabot, and A. Foster, "Teenage Fertility in Developed Nations: 1971–1980," *Family Planning Perspectives* 15 (1983):105–10.

[101] *Vital Statistics.*

[102] Ibid.

[103] U.S. Centers for Disease Control, "Premarital Sexual Experience among Adolescent Women: United States, 1970–1988," *Morbidity and Mortality Weekly Report* 39 (1991):929–32.

[104] K. Moore, *Facts at a Glance* (Washington, DC: Child Trends, Inc., 1990).

[105] Ibid., 1989.

[106] Ibid., 1990.

[107] Ibid.

[108] M. Dunkle, "Adolescent Pregnancy and Parenting: Evaluating School Policies and Programs from a Sex Equity Perspective" (Washington, DC: Council of Chief State School Officers Resource Center on Educational Equity, 1985); M. Nash and M. Dunkle, "The Need for a Warming Trend: A Survey of the School Climate for Pregnant and Parenting Teens" (Washington, DC: The Equality Center, 1989); M. Dunkle, "Keeping Mothers in School: Schools Today Aren't Making the Grade," *Public Welfare* (Summer 1990), pp. 9–14; Support Center for Educational Equity for Young Mothers, *Improving Educational Opportunities for Pregnant and Parenting Students: A Report on a Survey of Policies, Practices, Programs, and Plans for Pregnant and Parenting Students in Nine Urban School Districts* (New York: Academy for Educational Development, September 1988).

[109] J. Berrien et al., "Equal Educational Opportunities for Pregnant and Parenting Students: Meshing the Rights with the Realities" (New York: Women's Rights Project of the American Civil Liberties Union and the American Civil Liberties Union Foundation in cooperation with the American Association of University Women Educational Foundation and the American Association of University Women, 1990).

[110] Ibid.

[111] W. Marsiglio, "Teenage Fatherhood: High School Accreditation and Educational Attainment," in *Adolescent Fatherhood*, A. Elster and M. Lamb, eds. (Hillsdale, NJ: Lawrence Erlbaum Associates, 1986).

[112] Ibid.

[113] R. Parke and B. Neville, "Teenage Fatherhood," in *Risking the Future: Adolescent Sexuality, Pregnancy and Childbearing*, S. Hofferth and C. Hayes, eds., (Washington, DC: National Academy Press, 1987).

[114] Ibid.; also see F. Marx, S. Bailey, and J. Francis, *Child Care for the Children of Adolescent Parents: Findings from a National Survey and Case Studies*, Working Paper No. 184 (Wellesley College Center for Research on Women, 1988); J. Francis and F. Marx, *Learning Together: A National Directory of Teen Parenting and Child Care Programs* (Wellesley, MA: Wellesley College Center for Research on Women, 1989); F. Marx, *Learning Together: Supplement to the National Directory on Teen Parenting and Child Care Programs* (Wellesley, MA: Wellesley College Center for Research on Women, 1991); "Young Unwed Fathers and Welfare Reform," Family Impact Seminars (Washington, DC: American Association for Marriage and Family Therapy, Research and Education Foundation, November 18, 1988); "Teenage Parenthood, Poverty and Dependency: Do We Know How to Help?" Family Impact Seminars (Washington, DC: American Association for Marriage and Family Therapy, Research and Education Foundation, October 13, 1989); "Encouraging Unwed Fathers to be Responsible: Paternity Establishment, Child Support and JOBS Strategies," Family

Impact Seminars (Washington, DC: American Association for Marriage and Family Therapy, Research and Education Foundation, November 16, 1990).

115 M. Sullivan, *The Male Role in Teenage Pregnancy and Parenting: New Directions for Public Policy* (New York: Vera Institute of Justice, 1990).

116 F. Marx, *The Role of Day Care in Serving the Needs of School-Age Parents and Their Children: A Review of the Literature*, Working Paper No. 174 (Wellesley, MA: Wellesley College Center for Research on Women, 1987).

117 Marx, Bailey, and Francis, "Child Care"; see also Francis and Marx, *Learning Together: A National Directory*; Marx, *Learning Together: Supplement*; Nash and Dunkle, "Warming Trend"; Support Center for Educational Equity, *Educational Opportunities: A Report on Nine School Districts.*

118 J. Earle et al., *What's Promising: New Approaches to Dropout Prevention for Girls* (Alexandria, VA: National Association of State Boards of Education, 1987); see also J. Earle, V. Roach, and K. Fraser, *Female Dropouts: A New Perspective* (Alexandria, VA: National Association of State Boards of Education, 1987).

119 Ibid.

120 H. Ruch-Ross and E. Jones, "Comparing Effects of Teen Parent Programs," *The Ounce of Prevention Fund Magazine* (Spring 1988):9.

121 Marx, "The Role of Day Care."

122 Marx, Bailey, and Francis, "Child Care."

123 Ibid.

124 Federal involvement in vocational education began with the passage of the Smith-Hughes Act of 1917, which designated federal funds for vocational programs. In the 1960s federal policy began targeting resources to specific population groups such as the academically and economically disadvantaged, and the emotionally and physically disabled. While Title IX of the Education Amendments of 1972 focused on discrimination by sex in education programs, it was not until Title II of the Education Amendments of 1976 that specific requirements were placed on state vocational agencies regarding sex equity. Title II required all states to hire full-time personnel (usually referred to as sex-equity coordinators) to work toward the elimination of sex discrimination and sex stereotyping in vocational educational programs. The legislation also required states to develop programs for displaced homemakers, single heads of households, persons involuntarily working part-time, and those interested in nontraditional jobs. In spite of these specific requirements, federal law permitted considerable state-by-state variation in the kinds of vocational programs offered. A more complete discussion of the history of women in vocational education can be found in L. Vetter, "The Vocational Option for Women," in *Job Training for Women: The Promise and Limits of Public Policies*, S. Harlan and R. Steinberg, eds. (Philadelphia, PA: Temple University Press, 1989), pp. 91–113.

125 See J. Desy, P. Campbell, and J. Gardner, *High School Vocational Education Experiences: In School and in the Labor Market* (Columbus, OH: The National Center for Research in Vocational Education, Ohio State University, 1984); J. Grasso and J. Shea, *Vocational Education and Training: Impact on Youth* (Berkeley, CA: The Carnegie Council on Policy Studies in Higher Education, 1979); R. Rumberger and T. Daymont, *The Economic Value of Academic and Vocational Training Acquired in High School* (Stanford, CA: Institute for Research on Educational Finance and Governance, Stanford University, 1982).

126 P. Campbell et al., *Outcome of Vocational Education for Women, Minorities, the Handicapped and the Poor* (Columbus, OH: The National Center for Research in Vocational Education, Ohio State University, 1986).

127 Ibid.

128 L. Hargrave, W. Frazier, and T. Thomas, *Comprehensive Analysis of Follow-up*

Data for Students Enrolled in Traditional and Nontraditional Vocational and Technical Programs (Stillwater, OK: Oklahoma State Department of Vocational and Technical Education, 1983); I. Streker-Seeborg, M. Seeborg, and A. Zegeye, "The Impact of Nontraditional Training on the Occupational Attainment of Women," *The Journal of Human Resources* 19 (Fall 1984):452–71.

[129] Wirt et al., *Summary of Findings and Recommendations: National Assessment of Vocational Education* (Washington, DC: U.S. Department of Education, 1989).

[130] Ibid., p. 58.

[131] U.S. Department of Health and Human Services, National Center for Education Statistics, "Sex and Racial/Ethnic Characteristics of Full-Time Vocational Education Instructional Staff," Report No. NCES-82-207B, Washington, DC, [1982].

[132] Wirt et al., *National Assessment*, p. 50.

[133] Ibid.

[134] J. Mathews, "Faulty Figures Muddle Dropout Problem," *The Washington Post*, 2 June 1991, p. A-16.

[135] R. Rumberger, "High School Dropouts: A Review of the Issues and Evidence," *Review of Educational Research* 57 (1987):101—21.

[136] Ibid; V. Washington and J. Newman, "Setting Our Own Agenda: Exploring the Meaning of Gender Disparities among Blacks in Higher Education," *Journal of Negro Education* 60 (1991):19–35.

[137] T. McKenna and F. Ortiz, *The Broken Web, The Educational Experience of Hispanic American Women* (Berkeley, CA: Floricanto Press, 1988). There are also considerable differences by school type: Latina girls have significantly lower dropout rates in Catholic schools (8.2 percent) than in public schools (19.3 percent). Differences by type of school are also dramatic for black girls (1.8 percent drop out of Catholic schools versus 14.1 percent from public schools). While boys also drop out less in Catholic schools, differences are less dramatic than those for girls (a 70 per-cent difference for all boys versus an 83 percent differences for all girls). These data are for 1982 and are found in T. Hoffer, "Retention of Hispanic-American High School Youth," in McKenna and Ortiz, *The Broken Web*. This study did not report whether schools were single-sex or coeducational. However, another study of Catholic schools found significantly higher achievement levels for both girls and boys in single-sex schools, but particularly for girls. The larger effect for girls' schools was found in spite of higher per-pupil expenditures and a greater proportion of advantaged students in boys' schools. See V. Lee and A. Bryk, "Effects of Single-Sex Secondary Schools on Student Achievement and Attitudes," *Journal of Educational Psychology* 78 (1986):381–95.

[138] A. Kolstad and J. Owings, *High School Dropouts: What Changes Their Minds about School* (Washington, DC: Office of Educational Research and Improvement, U.S. Department of Education, 1986).

[139] U.S. Department of Commerce, Bureau of the Census, *Poverty in the United States*; 1988 and 1989, Series P-60, No. 171, p. 83.

[140] U.S. Commission on Civil Rights, *The Economic Status of Americans of Asian Descent: An Exploratory Investigation*, Clearinghouse Publication 95, October 1988.

[141] W. Morgan, "The High School Dropout in an Overeducated Society" (Columbus OH: Ohio State University, Center for Human Resources Research, February 1984).

[142] R. Ekstrom et al., "Who Drops Out and Why, Findings from a National Study," *Teachers College Record* 87 (1986):376.

[143] J. Earle, V. Roach, and K. Fraser for the Women's Equity Act Project, *Female Dropouts: A New Perspective* (Alexandria, VA: National Association of State Boards of Education, 1987), p. 9.

[144] Unpublished data from High School and Beyond, Washington, DC: U.S. Department of Education, 1982.

[145] R. Ekstrom et al., "Who Drops Out and Why." Data from the Hispanic Policy Development Project also reports that tenth-grade girls who expected to be married and/or mothers before age 20 had higher dropout rates.

[146] J. Dryfoos, *Adolescents at Risk: Prevalence and Prevention* (New York: Oxford University Press, 1990), p.102. See, for example, R. Tidwell, "Dropouts Speak Out: Qualitative Data on Early School Departure," *Adolescence* 23 (Winter 1988):940–54.

[147] M. Fine, *Framing Dropouts: Notes on the Politics of an Urban Public High School* (Albany, NY: State University Press of New York, 1991), p. 37.

[148] M. Fine and N. Zane, "Bein' Wrapped Too Tight: When Low Income Women Drop Out of High School," *Women's Studies Quarterly* 19 (Spring/Summer 1991):77–99, p. 81.

[149] Ibid.

PART THREE

....

[1] D. Rock et al., *Study of Excellence in High School Education: Longitudinal Study* (Princeton, NJ: Educational Testing Service, [1986]); M. Kimball, "A New Perspective on Women's Math Achievement," *Psychological Bulletin* 105 (1989).

[2] P. Rosser, *The SAT Gender Gap* (Washington, DC: Center for Women's Policy Studies, 1989).

[3] E. Diamond and C. Tittle, "Sex Equity in Testing," in *Handbook for Achieving Sex Equity Through Education*, S. Klein, ed. (Baltimore, MD: Johns Hopkins, 1985), p. 167.

[4] U.S. Congress, House Subcommittee on Civil and Constitutional Rights, *Fairness in Standardized Tests*, Testimony of C. Dwyer, Oversight Hearings, 100th Cong., 1st sess., 1987.

[5] Diamond and Tittle, "Sex Equity," p. 168.

[6] P. Selkow, *Assessing Sex Bias in Testing* (New York: Greenwood Press, 1984).

[7] U.S. Congress, House Subcommittee on Civil and Constitutional Rights, *Fairness in Standardized Tests*, Testimony of P. Rosser, Oversight Hearings, 100th Cong., 1st sess., 1987.

[8] C. Tittle, K. McCarthy, and J. Steckler, *Women and Educational Testing* (Princeton, NJ: Educational Testing Service, 1974).

[9] Q. McNemar, *The Revision of the Stanford-Binet Scale* (Boston, MA: Houghton Mifflin, 1942), p. 43.

[10] Ibid., p. 45.

[11] Ibid., p. 43.

[12] Rosser, *Gender Gap*, p. 71.

[13] T. Donlon and W. Angoff, "The Scholastic Aptitude Test," in *The College Board Admissions Testing Program*, W. Angoff, ed. (New York: College Entrance Examination Board, 1971), pp. 25–26.

[14] M. Clark and J. Grandy, *Sex Differences in the Academic Performance of Scholastic Aptitude Test Takers* (New York: College Entrance Examination Board, 1984), p. 1.

[15] Ibid., p. 23.

[16] A. Harris and S. Carlton, "Patterns of Gender Differences on Mathematics Items on the Scholastic Aptitude Test," paper presented at the annual meeting of the American Educational Research Association, Boston, MA, April 1990.

[17] S. Chipman, "Cognitive Issues in Math

Test Bias," paper presented at the annual meeting of the American Educational Research Association, New Orleans, LA, April 1988; J. Hyde, E. Fennema, and S. Lamon, "Gender Differences in Mathematics Performance: A Math Analysis," *Psychological Bulletin* 107, no. 2 (1990):139–55.

[18] Harris and Carlton, "Patterns of Gender Differences."

[19] Rosser, *Gender Gap.*

[20] Mullis et al., *Women and Minorities in Science and Engineering* (Washington, DC: National Science Foundation, 1990).

[21] C. Wendler and S. Carlton, "An Examination of SAT Verbal Items for Differential Performance by Women and Men: An Exploratory Study," paper presented at the annual meeting of the American Educational Research Association, Washington, DC, April 1987.

[22] M. Linn and J. Hyde, "Gender, Mathematics and Science," *Educational Researcher* 18 (November 1989):17–27; Wendler and Carlton, "SAT Verbal Items."

[23] Rosser, *Gender Gap.*

[24] Ibid.; J. Loewen, P. Rosser, and J. Katzman, "Gender Bias on SAT Items," paper presented at the annual meeting of the American Education Research Association, New Orleans, LA, April 1988.

[25] Burton, "Trends in Verbal Scores."

[26] J. McLarty, C. Nobel, and R. Huntley, "Effects of Item Wording on Sex Bias," paper presented to the National Council on Measurement in Education, New Orleans, LA, April 1988, p. 20.

[27] S. Chipman, S. Marshall, and P. Scott, "Content Effects on Word Problem Performance as a Possible Source of Test Bias," *American Educational Research Journal* 28 (1991):897–915.

[28] Harris and Carlton, "Patterns of Gender Differences."

[29] S. Chipman, "Word Problems Where Test Bias Creeps In," paper presented at the annual meeting of the American

Educational Research Association, New Orleans, LA, April 1988, p. 24.

[30] J. Mazzeo, A. Schmitt, and C. Bleistein, "Do Women Perform Better, Relative to Men, on Constructed Response Tests or Multiple Choice Tests? Evidence from the Advanced Placement Examinations," paper presented at the meeting of the National Council on Measurement in Education, Chicago, IL, April 1991; N. Peterson and S. Livingston, *English Composition Test with Essay: A Descriptive Study of the Relationship Between Essay and Objective Scores by Ethnic Group and Sex* (Princeton, NJ: Education Testing Service, [1982]).

[31] B. Becker, "Item Characteristics and Gender Differences on the SAT-M for Mathematically Able Youths," *American Educational Research Journal* 27 no. 1 (1990); Linn et al., "Gender Differences in National Assessment of Educational Progress Science Items: What does 'I Don't Know' really mean?" *Journal of Research in Science Teaching* 24, no. 3 (1987):267–78.

[32] B. Becker, "Item Characteristics and Gender Differences on the SAT-M."

[33] M. Pearlman, "Trends in Women's Total Score and Item Performance on Verbal Measures," paper presented at the annual meeting of the American Educational Research Association, Washington, DC, April 1987; Wendler and Carlton, "SAT Verbal Items."

[34] J. Loewen, P. Rosser, and J. Katzman, "Gender Bias in SAT Items," paper presented at the annual meeting of the American Educational Research Association, New Orleans, LA, 1988; Wendler and Carlton, "SAT Verbal Items."

[35] Linn et al., "Gender Differences."

[36] R. Hembree, "Correlates, Causes, Effects and Treatment of Test Anxiety," *Review of Educational Research* 38, no. 1 (1988).

[37] Loewen, Rosser, and Katzman, "Gender Bias."

[38] Linn et al., "Gender Differences."

[39] B. Bridgeman and C. Wendler, *Prediction*

of Grades in College Mathematics Courses as a Component of the Placement Validity of SAT-Mathematics Scores (New York: College Board, 1989); Loewen, Rosser, and Katzman, "Gender Bias"; E. Rodgers and A. Stenta, "Effects of Improving the Reliability of the GPA on Prediction Generally and on Comparative Predictions for Gender and Race Particularly," Journal of Educational Measurement 25, no. 4 (1988); Clark and Grandy, "Sex Differences," p. 1.

[40] Bridgeman and Wendler, "Prediction of Grades."

[41] R. McCormack and M. McLeod, "Gender Bias in the Prediction of College Course Performance," Journal of Educational Measurement 25, no. 4 (1988):321–32; Bridgeman and Wendler, "Prediction of Grades."

[42] H. Wainer and L. Steinberg, Sex Differences in Performance on the Mathematics Section of the Scholastic Aptitude Test: A Biodirectional Validity Study (Princeton, NJ: Educational Testing Service, 1990), p. 7.

[43] ACT, Assessment Results: 1990 National Summary Report (Iowa City, IA: American College Testing [1990]).

[44] Researcher Morton Slater to section coauthor Patricia B. Campbell, 30 May 1991.

[45] E. Diamond, "Gender Bias in Testing: An Overview," paper presented at the hearing on gender bias in testing cosponsored by National Women's Law Center and National Commission on Testing and Public Policy, Washington, DC, October 1989.

[46] M. Zieky, "Are Performance Tests for Teacher Certification Less Biased Than Paper and Pencil Tests?" paper presented at the annual meeting of the American Educational Research Association, San Francisco, CA, April 1989.

[47] P. Murphy, "What Has Been Learnt About Assessment from the Work of the APU Science Project?" in The Assessment of Hands-on Elementary Science Projects, G. Hein, ed. (Grand Forks, ND: University of North Dakota: Center for Teaching and Learning, 1990), p. 168.

[48] Ibid.

[49] Ibid., p. 170.

PART FOUR

Chapter 1

[1] We analyze these reports in Part One. None examines curriculum content in depth. Recently, however, the leaders of more than thirty-three national subject-matter groups met to form an organization devoted to putting curricular issues at the top of the education-reform agenda. This effort promises to call attention to the central position of curriculum in schooling. "Alliance Formed to Push Curriculum to Front of Reform Agenda," *Education Week*, September 4, 1991, p. 14.

[2] M. Sadker, D. Sadker, and S. Steindam, "Gender Equity and Education Reform," *Educational Leadership* 46, no. 6 (1989):44–47. See also M. Tetreault and P. Schmuck, "Equity, Education Reform, and Gender," *Issues in Education* 3, no. 1 (1985):45–67.

[3] K. Bogart, *Solutions That Work: Identification and Elimination of Barriers to the Participation of Female and Minority Students in Academic Educational Programs*, 3 vols. and User's Manual (Washington, DC: National Education Association, forthcoming). The three ongoing national faculty-development programs that focus on creation of gender-fair curriculum in K–12 classes in humanities and social studies are the National Women's History Project, Windsor, CA; the Harvard Graduate School of Education, Summer Institutes on "American History: The Female Experience"; and the multidisciplinary National SEED Project (Seeking Educational Equity and Diversity) of the Wellesley College Center for Research on Women. The Educational Materials and Service Center of Edmonds, WA, and the GESA Program (Gender Expectations and Student Achievement) of the Graymill Foundation, Earlham, IA,

offer equity training that bears indirectly on course content.

[4] For general reviews of curriculum research, see P. Arlow and C. Froschl, "Textbook Analysis," in F. Howe, ed., *High School Feminist Studies* (Old Westbury, NY: The Feminist Press, 1976), pp. xi–xxviii. K. Scott and C. Schau, "Sex Equity and Sex Bias in Instructional Materials," and P. Blackwell and L. Russo, "Sex Equity Strategies in the Content Areas," in S. Klein, ed., *Handbook for Achieving Sex Equity Through Education*, (Baltimore, MD: Johns Hopkins University Press, 1985), pp. 218–60; M. Hulme, "Mirror, Mirror on the Wall: Biased Reflections in Textbooks and Instructional Materials," in A. Carelli, ed., *Sex Equity in Education: Readings and Strategies* (Springfield, IL: Charles C. Thomas, 1988), pp. 187–208.

[5] *Dick and Jane As Victims: Sex Stereotyping in Children's Readers* (Princeton, NJ: Women on Words and Images, 1975); *Help Wanted: Sexism in Career Education Materials* (Princeton, NJ: Women on Words and Images, 1976) and *Sexism in Foreign Language Texts* (Princeton, NJ: Women on Words and Images, 1976). See also L. Weitzman and D. Rizzo, *Biased Textbooks and Images of Males and Females in Elementary School Textbooks* (Washington, DC: Resource Center on Sex Roles in Education, 1976); G. Britton and M. Lumpkin, *A Consumer's Guide to Sex, Race, and Career Bias in Public School Textbooks* (Corvallis, OR: Britton Associates, 1977).

[6] J. Trecker, "Women in U.S. History High School Textbooks," *Social Education* 35, no. 3 (1971):249–60, 338.

[7] O. Davis et al., "A Review of U.S. History Textbooks," *The Education Digest* 52, no. 3 (November 1986):50–53; M. Hitchcock and G. Tompkins, "Basal Readers: Are

They Still Sexist?" *The Reading Teacher* 41, no. 3 (December 1987):288–92; M. Tetreault, "Integrating Women's History: The Case of United States History High School Textbooks," *The History Teacher* 19 (February 1986):211–62; M. Tetreault, "The Journey from Male-Defined to Gender-Balanced Education," *Theory into Practice* 25, no. 4 (Autumn 1986):227–34; A. Nilsen, "Three Decades of Sexism in School Science Materials," *School Library Journal* 34, no. 1 (September 1987):117–22; E. Hall, "One Week for Women? The Structure of Inclusion of Gender Issues in Introductory Textbooks," *Teaching Sociology* 16, no. 4 (October 1988):431–42; P. Purcell and L. Stewart, "Dick and Jane in 1989," *Sex Roles* 22, nos. 3 and 4 (February 1990):177–85.

[8] A. Applebee, *A Study of Book-Length Works Taught in High School English Courses* (Albany, NY: Center for the Learning and Teaching of Literature, State University of New York School of Education, 1989).

[9] Ibid., p. 18.

[10] P. Campbell and J. Wirtenberg, "How Books Influence Children: What the Research Shows," *Interracial Books for Children Bulletin* 11, no. 6 (1980):3–6.

[11] At its highest level of support in 1980, the Office of Education spent only .2 percent of its budget on sex equity. Subsequently, however, the Reagan administration attempted unsuccessfully to reduce to "zero budget" the two largest programs supporting race and sex equity, the Title IV programs of the Civil Rights Act and the Women's Educational Equity Act. The sense that race equity and sex equity programs figured in a federal agenda diminished. This disinvestment is reflected by the absence of sex, gender, and cultural awareness in most of the national reports of the late 1980s. See K. Levy, *What's Left of Federal Funding for Sex Equity in Education and Social Science Research?* (Tempe, AZ: Arizona State University Publications Office, 1985).

[12] Initiatives have included classroom innovations by thousands of individual teachers, conferences, and summer institutes for teachers at the University of Arizona, University of New Hampshire, Dana Hall School, and Ohio State University. The National Coalition for Sex Equity in Education (NCSEE) developed an active network of equity professionals. Further efforts have also included the forming of women's caucuses in professional organizations; workshops and materials from the National Women's History Project; dissemination of syllabi and bibliographies; new journals including *Feminist Teacher*; special focus sections of journals, for example, *English Journal* 77, no. 6 (October 1988), 78, no. 6 (October 1989); inservice activities sponsored by local school boards and districts, and aid from ten federal Equity Assistance Centers. Despite decreased funding, the Women's Education Equity Act Program continues to fund projects and to support the dissemination of materials via the WEEA Publishing Center at the Educational Development Center in Newton, MA.

[13] Scott and Schau, "Sex Equity and Sex Bias," p. 226. See also the discussion by B. Wright in "The Feminist Transformation of Foreign Language Teaching," in M. Burkhard and E. Waldstein, eds., *Women in German Yearbook 1* (Lanham, MD: University Press of America, 1985), pp. 95–97. Wright lists thirteen publishing houses that issued guidelines between 1972 and 1981 on avoiding or eliminating sex stereotypes. She discusses problems of noncompliance, as well as the limits of strategies for elimination of simple sex stereotyping in the face of larger problems such as overwhelmingly masculine and/or elite perspectives in texts as a whole.

[14] M. Tetreault, "Integrating Women's History: The Case of U.S. History High School Textbooks," *The History Teacher* 19 (February 1986):211–62; "Women in the Curriculum," *Comment on Conferences and Research on Women* (February 1986):1–2; "Rethinking Women, Gender, and the Social Studies," *Social Education* 51 (March 1987):171–78.

[15] Newsletter of the Special Interest Group

on Gender and Social Justice, National Council for Social Studies, December 1990.

[16] Surveys were taken in the Andrew W. Mellon, Geraldine Rockefeller Dodge, Kentucky, and National SEED Project Seminars for College and School Teachers, sponsored by the Wellesley College Center for Research on Women. Twenty U.S. history textbooks were analyzed each year with regard to the representation of women as authors/editors and subjects in text and illustrations and the representation of domains of life outside of war, law, policy, government, and management of public affairs.

[17] Homework assignments and study questions given in textbooks most frequently depend on the type of knowing which the authors of *Women's Ways of Knowing* identify as "separated," in which the mode is detached or distant from the subject. Girls and women, in a study of students in six schools and colleges, preferred a mode of knowing that the investigators named "connected," which involves empathetic identification with the subject. The investigators call for more "connected teaching," in which the capacity for identification is seen as an aspect of knowing and of learning about course content. M. Belenky et al., *Women's Ways of Knowing* (New York: Basic Books, 1986), pp. 100–30, 214–29.

[18] See B. Wright, "What's in a Noun? A Feminist Perspective on Foreign Language Instruction," *Women's Studies Quarterly* 12, no. 3 (Fall 1984):2–6; B. Schmitz, "Guidelines for Reviewing Foreign Language Textbooks for Sex Bias," *Women's Studies Quarterly* 12, no. 3 (Fall 1984):7–9.

[19] L. Pinkle, "Language Learning from a Feminist Perspective: Selected College-Level Grammar Textbooks," *Women's Studies Quarterly* 12, no. 3 (Fall 1984): 10–13. Since 1985, *The Women in German Yearbook* (Lanham, MD: University Press of America) has published periodic reviews of research on instructional materials for German courses, including high school texts. The most recent review was published in the Spring 1991 issue: "Frauen/Unterricht: Feminist Reviews of Teaching Materials," L. French. K. Von Ankum, and M. Webster, eds.

[20] Bogart, *Solutions That Work*, vol. 3, pp. 107–108.

[21] E. Style, "Curriculum As Window and Mirror," in *Listening for All Voices: Gender Balancing the School Curriculum* (Summit, NJ: Oak Knoll School, 1988), pp. 6–12.

[22] Surveys were taken in the Andrew W. Mellon, Geraldine Rockefeller Dodge, Kentucky, and National SEED Project Seminars for college and school teachers, sponsored by the Wellesley College Center for Research on Women.

[23] G. Wilbur, "Gender-fair Curriculum," research report prepared for Wellesley College Research on Women, August 1991.

[24] National Council of Teachers of Mathematics, *Curriculum and Evaluation Standards for School Mathematics* (Reston, VA: National Council of Teachers of Mathematics, 1989).

[25] Ibid., p. 17.

[26] F. Rutherford and A. Ahlgren, *Science for All Americans* (New York: Oxford University Press, 1989), pp. 204–14.

[27] J. Banks, "Integrating the Curriculum with Ethnic Content: Approaches and Guidelines," in J. Banks and C. Banks, eds., *Multicultural Education: Issues and Perspectives* (Boston, MA: Allyn and Bacon, 1989), pp. 192–207.

[28] P. McIntosh, *Interactive Phases of Curricular Re-Vision: A Feminist Perspective*, Working Paper No. 124 (Wellesley MA: Wellesley College Center for Research on Women, 1983). For further typologies in phase theory, see M. Schuster and S. Van Dyne, eds., *Women's Place in the Academy: Transforming the Liberal Arts* (Totawa, NJ: Rowman and Allanheld, 1985; and M. Tetreault, "Feminist Phase Theory: An Experience-Derived Evaluation Model," *Journal of Higher Education* 56 (July–August 1985); and "Integrating

Content about Women and Gender into the Curriculum," in Banks and Banks, eds., *Multicultural Education*, pp. 124–44. See also *Comment on Conferences and Research on Women* 15, no. 2, Claremont, CA, February 1986, pp. 1–4; P. McIntosh, *Interactive Phases of Curricular and Personal Re-Vision With Regard to Race*, Working Paper No. 219 (Wellesley, MA: Wellesley College Center for Research on Women, 1990), p. 6.

29 "Stages of Curriculum Transformation," in M. Schuster and S. Van Dyne, eds., *Women's Place in the Academy: Transforming the Liberal Arts Curriculum* (Totowa, NJ: Rowman & Allanheld Publishers, 1985), pp. 13–29; M. Tetreault, "Women in U.S. History—Beyond a Patriarchal Perspective," *Interracial Books for Children Bulletin* 11 (1980):F-10; McIntosh, *Interactive Phases of Curricular Re-Vision*. See also M. Belenky et al., *Women's Ways of Knowing* (New York: Basic Books, Inc., 1986); C. Gilligan, *In a Different Voice* (Cambridge, MA: Harvard University Press, 1982); E. Minnich, *Transforming Knowledge* (Philadelphia, PA: Temple University Press, 1990).

30 P. McIntosh, *Interactive Phases of Curricular and Personal Re-Vision With Regard to Race*, Working Paper No. 219 (Wellesley, MA: Wellesley College Center for Research on Women, 1990), p. 6.

31 Gilligan, *In a Different Voice*.

32 Bogart, *Solutions That Work*, vol. 1, pp. 97–98.

33 T. Kidder, *Among Schoolchildren* (New York: Avon Books, 1989), p. 27.

34 A. Applebee, *A Study of Book-Length Works*, p. 18. For an example of a product that came out of a school-based departmental discussion, see *New Voices for the English Classroom*, C. Peter, ed., (Providence, RI: Lincoln School, 1986). For similar strategies, see E. Style, *Multicultural Education and Me*, and the school-based, teacher-led seminars established through the National SEED Project on Inclusive Curriculum, Wellesley College Center for Research on Women.

35 State of New York, Education Department, *One Nation, Many Peoples: A Declaration of Cultural Interdepen-dence, The Report of the New York State Social Studies Review and Development Committee, June 1991*, pp. 18–126. See also memos of July 12 and 15 from Commissioner T. Sobol to the Board of Regents.

36 C. Nelson, "Gender and the Social Studies: Training Preservice Secondary Social Studies Teachers" (Ph.D. diss., University of Minnesota, 1990), pp. 8, 38–39.

37 L. Kerber, "'Opinionative Assurance': The Challenge of Women's History," address to the Organization of History Teachers, American Historical Association, New York, NY, 28 December 1990, p. 11.

Chapter 2

1 See for example, J. Brophy and T. Good, *Teacher-Student Relationships: Causes and Consequences* (New York: Holt, Rinehart, and Winston, 1974); M. Jones, "Gender Bias in Classroom Interactions," *Contemporary Education* 60 (Summer 1989):216–22; M. Lockheed, *Final Report: A Study of Sex Equity in Classroom Interaction* (Washington, DC: National Institute of Education, 1984); M. Lockheed and A. Harris, *Classroom Interaction and Opportunities for Cross-Sex Peer Learning in Science*, paper presented at the Annual Meeting of the American Educational Research Association, New York, April 1989; M. Sadker and D. Sadker, "Sexism in the Classroom: From Grade School to Graduate School," *Phi Delta Kappan* 68 (1986):512; R. Spaulding, *Achievement, Creativity and Self-Concept Correlates of Teacher-Pupil Transactions in Elementary School* (Cooperative Research Project No. 1352), (Washington, DC: U.S. Department of Health Education and Welfare, 1963).

2 L. Serbin et al., "A Comparison of Teacher Responses to the Pre-Academic and Problem Behavior of Boys and Girls," *Child Development* 44 (1973):796–804;

M. Ebbeck, "Equity for Boys and Girls: Some Important Issues," *Early Child Development and Care* 18 (1984):119–31.

[3] M. Sadker and D. Sadker, "Sexism in the Classroom: From Grade School to Graduate School," *Phi Delta Kappan* 68 (1986):513; M. Sadker and D. Sadker, "Is the OK Classroom OK?" *Phi Delta Kappan* 55 (1985):361.

[4] J. Brophy, "Teacher Praise: A Functional Analysis," *Review of Educational Research* 51 (1981):5-32; A. Gardner, C. Mason, and M. Matyas, "Equity, Excellence and 'Just Plain Good Teaching!'" *The American Biology Teacher* 51 (1989):72–77.

[5] M. Sadker and D. Sadker, *Year 3: Final Report, Promoting Effectiveness in Classroom Instruction* (Washington, DC: National Institute of Education, 1984).

[6] D. Baker, "Sex Differences in Classroom Interactions in Secondary Science," *Journal of Classroom Interaction* 22 (1986): 212–18; J. Becker, "Differential Treatment of Females and Males in Mathematics Classes," *Journal for Research in Mathematics Education* 12 (1981):40–53; L. Berk and N. Lewis, "Sex Role and Social Behavior in Four School Environments," *Elementary School Journal* 3 (1977):205–21; L. Morse and H. Handley, "Listening to Adolescents: Gender Differences in Science Classroom Interaction," in *Gender Influences in Classroom Interaction,* L. Wilkerson and C. Marrett, eds. (Orlando, FL: Academic Press, 1985), pp. 37–56.

[7] M. Seligman and S. Maier, "Failure to Escape Traumatic Shock," *Journal of Experimental Psychology* 74 (1967):1–9.

[8] C. Dweck and N. Repucci, "Learned Helplessness and Reinforcement Responsibility in Children," *Journal of Personality and Social Psychology* 25 (1973):109–16; C. Dweck and T. Goetz, "Attributions and Learned Helplessness," in *New Directions in Attribution Research,* J. Harvey, W. Ickes, and R. Kidd, eds. (Hillsdale, NJ: Erlbaum, 1978).

[9] See for example, K. Deaux, "Sex: A Perspective on the Attribution Process," in *New Directions in Attribution Research;* C. Dweck and E. Bush, "Sex Differences in Learned Helplessness: I. Differential Debilitation with Peer and Adult Evaluators," *Developmental Psychology* 12 (1976):147–56; C. Dweck, T. Goetz, and N. Strauss, "Sex Differences in Learned Helplessness: IV. An Experimental and Naturalistic Study of Failure Generalization and Its Mediators," *Journal of Personality and Social Psychology* 38 (1980):441–52; L. Reyes, *Mathematics Classroom Processes,* paper presented at the Fifth International Congress on Mathematical Education, Adelaide, Australia, August 1984; P. Wolleat et al., "Sex Differences in High School Students' Causal Attributions of Performance in Mathematics," *Journal for Research in Mathematics Education* 11 (1980):356–66; D. Phillips, "The Illusion of Incompetence among Academically Competent Children," *Child Development* 55 (1984):2000–16; E. Fennema et al., "Teachers' Attributions and Belief about Girls, Boys, and Mathematics," *Educational Studies in Mathematics* 21 (1990):55–69.

[10] E. Maccoby and C. Jacklin, *The Psychology of Sex Differences* (Stanford, CA: Stanford University Press, 1974); E. Lenney, "Women's Self-Confidence in Achievement Settings," *Psychological Bulletin* 84 (1977):1–13; J. Parsons and D. Ruble, "The Development of Achievement-Related Expectancies," *Child Development* 48 (1977):1075–79; Dweck, Goetz, and Strauss, "Sex Differences in Learned Helplessness: IV"; J. Goetz, "Children's Sex Role Knowledge and Behavior: An Ethnographic Study of First Graders in the Rural South," *Theory and Research in Social Education* 8 (1981):31–54.

[11] W. Shepard and D. Hess, "Attitudes in Four Age Groups Toward Sex Role Division in Adult Occupations and Activities," *Journal of Vocational Behavior* 6 (1975):27–39; C. Dweck and E. Elliot, "Achievement Motivation," in *Handbook of Child Psychology,* vol. 4, P. Mussen and E. Hetherington, eds. (New York: Wiley, 1983); R. Felson, "The Effect of Self-Appraisals of Ability on Academic

Performance," *Journal of Personality and Social Psychology* 47 (1984):944–52; M. Stewart and C. Corbin, "Feedback Dependence among Low Confidence Preadolescent Boys and Girls," *Research Quarterly for Exercise and Sport* 59 (1988):160–64.

12 J. Eccles-Parsons et al., "Sex Differences in Attributions and Learned Helplessness," *Sex Roles* 8 (1982):421–32; J. Eccles-Parsons, C. Kaczala, and J. Meece, "Socialization of Achievement Attitudes and Beliefs: Classroom Influences," *Child Development* 53 (1982):322–39; J. Eccles, "Expectancies, Values and Academic Behaviors," in *Achievement and Achievement Motives*, J. Spence, ed. (San Francisco, CA: W.H. Freeman and Co., 1983); J. Eccles, *Understanding Motivation: Achievement Beliefs, Gender-Roles and Changing Educational Environments*, address before American Psychological Association, New York, 1987.

13 B. Licht, S. Stader, and C. Swenson, "Children's Achievement Related Beliefs: Effects of Academic Area, Sex, and Achievement Level," *Journal of Educational Research* 82 (1989):253–60.

14 J. Kahle, "Why Girls Don't Know," in *What Research Says to the Science Teacher— the Process of Knowing*, M. Rowe, ed. (Washington, DC: National Science Testing Association, 1990), pp. 55–67; V. Lee, "Sexism in Single-Sex and Coeducational Secondary School Classrooms," paper presented at the annual meeting of the American Sociological Association, Cincinnati, OH, August 8, 1991.

15 J. Eccles, "Bringing Young Women to Math and Science," in *Gender and Thought: Psychological Perspectives*, M. Crawford and M. Gentry, eds. (New York: Springer-Verlag, 1989), pp. 36–58; Licht et al., "Children's Achievement Related Beliefs."

16 Sadker and Sadker, *Year 3*; L. Grant, "Race-Gender Status, Classroom Interaction and Children's Socialization in Elementary School," in *Gender Influences in Classroom Interaction*, L. Wilkinson and C. Marrett, eds. (Orlando, FL: Academic

Press, 1985), pp. 57–75.

17 Grant, "Race-Gender Status," p.66.

18 C. Cornbleth and W. Korth, "Teacher Perceptions and Teacher-Student Interaction in Integrated Classrooms," *Journal of Experimental Education* 48 (Summer 1980):259–63; B. Hare, *Black Girls: A Comparative Analysis of Self-Perception and Achievement by Race, Sex and Socioeconomic Background*, Report No. 271, (Baltimore, MD: John Hopkins University, Center for Social Organization of Schools, [1979]).

19 S. Damico and E. Scott, "Behavior Differences Between Black and White Females in Desegregated Schools," *Equity and Excellence* 23 (1987):63–66; Grant, "Race-Gender Status." See also J. Irvine, "Teacher-Student Interactions: Effects of Student Race, Sex, and Grade Level," *Journal of Educational Psychology* 78 (1986):14–21.

20 Damico and Scott, "Behavior Differences"; Hare, "Black Girls: A Comparative Analysis."

21 Damico and Scott, "Behavior Differences"; L. Grant, "Black Females 'Place' in Integrated Classrooms," *Sociology of Education* 57 (1984):98–111.

22 Damico and Scott, "Behavior Differences."

23 D. Scott-Jones and M. Clark, "The School Experience of Black Girls: The Interaction of Gender, Race and Socioeconomic Status," *Phi Delta Kappan* 67 (March 1986):20–526.

24 V. Washington and J. Newman, "Setting Our Own Agenda: Exploring the Meaning of Gender Disparities Among Blacks in Higher Education," *Journal of Negro Education* 60 (1991):19–35.

25 E. Fennema and P. Peterson, "Effective Teaching for Girls and Boys: The Same or Different?" in *Talks to Teachers*, D. Berliner and B. Rosenshine, eds. (New York: Random House, 1987), pp. 111–25; J. Stallings, "School Classroom and Home Influences on Women's Decisions to Enroll in Advanced Mathematics Courses," in

Women and Mathematics: Balancing the Equation, S. Chipman, L. Brush, and D. Wilson, eds. (Hillsdale, NJ: Erlbaum, 1985), pp. 199–224; S. Greenberg, "Educational Equity in Early Education Environments," in Handbook for Achieving Sex Equity Through Education, S. Klein, ed. (Baltimore, MD: John Hopkins University Press, 1985), pp.457–69.

26 D. Baker, "Sex Differences in Classroom Interactions in Secondary Science," Journal of Classroom Interaction 22 (1986): 212–18.

27 D. Jorde and A. Lea, "The Primary Science Project in Norway," in Proceedings of Growth GSAT Conference, J. Kahle, J. Daniels, and J. Harding, eds. (West Lafayette, IN: Purdue University, 1987), pp. 66–72.

28 P. Flores, "How Dick and Jane Perform Differently in Geometry: Test Results on Reasoning, Visualization and Affective Factors," paper presented at American Educational Research Association Meeting, Boston, MA, April 1990.

29 J. Kahle, Factors Affecting the Retention of Girls in Science Courses and Careers: Case Studies of Selected Secondary Schools (Reston, VA: The National Association of Biology Teachers, October 1983).

30 Eccles, "Bringing Young Women to Math and Science."

31 M. Belenky et al., Women's Ways of Knowing: The Development of Self, Body, and Mind (New York: Basic Books, Inc., 1986).

32 G. Engelhard and J. Monsaas, "Academic Performance, Gender and the Cooperative Attitudes of Third, Fifth and Seventh Graders," Journal of Research and Development in Education 22 (1989):13–17.

33 A. Ahlgren and D. Johnson, "Sex Differences in Cooperative and Competitive Attitudes from 2nd Through the 12th Grades," Developmental Psychology 15 (1979):45–49; B. Herndon and M. Carpenter, "Sex Differences in Cooperative and Competitive Attitudes in a Northeastern School," Psychological Reports 50 (1982): 768–70; L. Owens and R. Straton, "The

Development of Co-operative Competitive and Individualized Learning Preference Scale for Students," Journal of Educational Psychology 50 (1980):147–61.

34 S. Sharon et al., eds., Cooperation in Education (Provo, UT: Brigham Young University Press, 1980); S. Bossert, Task Structure and Social Relationships (Cambridge, MA: Harvard University Press, 1979); W. Shrum, N. Cheek, and S. Hunter, "Friendship in the School: Gender and Racial Homophily," Sociology of Education 61 (1988):227–39.

35 E. Aronson, The Jigsaw Classroom (Beverly Hills, CA: Sage, 1978); D. DeVries and K. Edwards, "Student Teams and Learning Games: Their Effects on Cross-Race and Cross-Sex Interaction," Journal of Educational Psychology 66 (1974):741–49; P. Okebukola, "Cooperative Learning and Students' Attitude to Laboratory Work," Social Science and Mathematics 86 (1986):582–90; R. Slavin, "How Student Learning Teams Can Integrate the Desegregated Classroom," Integrated Education 15 (1977):56–58.

36 N. Blaney et al., "Interdependence in the Classroom: A Field Study," Journal of Educational Psychology 69 (1977):121–28; D. DeVries and K. Edwards, "Student Teams and Learning Games"; Sharon et al., Cooperation in Education; R. Slavin, "Cooperative Learning," Review of Educational Research 50 (1980):315–42; R. Slavin, "Cooperative Learning and Desegregation," in W. Hawley, ed., Effective School Desegregation (Berkeley, CA: Sage, 1981); R. Weigle, P. Wiser, and S. Cook, "The Impact of Cooperative Learning Experiences on Cross-Ethnic Relations and Attitude," Journal of Social Issues 3 (1975):219–44.

37 M. Hallinan, The Evolution of Children's Friendship Cliques (ERIC Document Reproduction Service no. ED 161556, 1977); R. Best, We've All Got Scars: What Boys and Girls Learn in Elementary School (Bloomington, IN: University Press, 1983); J. Eccles-Parsons, "Sex Differences in Mathematics Participation," in M. Steinkamp and M. Maehr, eds., Women in Science

(Greenwich, CT: JAI Press, 1984); M. Hallinan and N. Tumma, "Classroom Effects on Change in Children," *Sociology of Education* 51 (1978):170–282.

[38] M. Lockheed, K. Finklestein, and A. Harris, *Curriculum and Research for Equity: Model Data Package* (Princeton, NJ: Educational Testing Service, 1979).

[39] B. Eakins and R. Eakins, "Sex Roles, Interruptions, and Silences in Conversation," in B. Thorne and N. Henley, eds., *Sex Differences in Human Communication* (Boston, MA: Houghton Mifflin, 1978); N. Henley and B. Thorne, "Women Speak and Men Speak: Sex Differences and Sexism in Communications, Verbal and Nonverbal," in A. Sargent, ed., *Beyond Sex Roles* (St. Paul, MN: West Publishing Company, 1977); R. Lakoff, *Languages and Women's Place* (New York: Harper Colophon Books, 1976); D. Tannen, *You Just Don't Understand: Women and Men in Conversation* (New York: William Morrow, 1990).

[40] L. Wilkinson, J. Lindow, and C. Chiang, "Sex Differences and Sex Segregation in Students' Small-Group Communication," in L. Wilkinson and C. Marret, eds., *Gender Influences in Classroom Interaction* (Orlando, FL: Academic Press, 1985), pp. 185–207.

[41] J. Berger, T. Conner, and M. Fisek, eds., *Expectation States Theory: A Theoretical Research Program* (Cambridge, MA: Winthrop, 1974); M. Lockheed and A. Harris, "Cross-Sex Collaborative Learning in Elementary Classrooms," *American Educational Research Journal* 21 (1984):275–94.

[42] Lockheed and Harris, "Cross-Sex Collaborative Learning."

[43] C. Weisfeld et al., "The Spelling Bee: A Naturalistic Study of Female Inhibitions in Mixed-Sex Competitions," *Adolescence* 18 (1983):695–708.

[44] For example, M. Lockheed and A. Harris, "Classroom Interaction and Opportunity for Cross-Sex Peer Learning in Science," *Journal of Early Adolescence* (1982):135–43.

[45] S. Strauss, "Sexual Harassment in the School: Legal Implications for Principals," *National Association of Secondary School Principals Bulletin* (1988):93–97; N. Stein, ed., *Who's Hurt and Who's Liable: Sexual Harassment in Massachusetts Schools*, 4th ed. (Quincy, MA: Massachusetts Department of Education, 1986).

[46] D. Grayson, "Emerging Equity Issues Related to Homosexuality," *Peabody Journal of Education* 64 (1989):132–45.

Chapter 3

[1] R. Jessor, "Risk Behavior in Adolescence: A Psychosocial Framework for Understanding and Action," paper prepared for Cornell University Medical College Conference "Adolescents at Risk: Medical and Social Perspectives," Cornell University, February 1991; J. Dryfoos, *Youth at Risk: Prevalence and Prevention* (Oxford: Oxford University Press, 1990).

[2] *Preventing Adolescent Pregnancy: What Schools Can Do* (Washington, DC: Children's Defense Fund, 1986).

[3] Dryfoos, *Youth at Risk*, p. 107.

[4] J. Earle and V. Roach, "Female Dropouts: A New Perspective," in *Women's Educational Equity Act Publishing Center Digest* (Newton, MA: Education Development Center, 1988); M. Fine, *Framing Dropouts* (Albany, NY: State University of New York Press, 1991).

[5] J. Gans and D. Blyth, *America's Adolescents: How Healthy Are They?* (Chicago, IL: American Medical Association, 1990), p. 28.

[6] H. Adger, "Problems of Alcohol and Other Drug Use and Abuse in Adolescence," paper prepared for Cornell University Medical College Conference "Adolescents at Risk: Medical and Social Perspectives," Cornell University, February 1991.

[7] *Facts and Reflections on Girls and Substance Use* (New York: Girls Clubs of America, Inc., 1988), p. 9.

[8] Adger, "Problems of Alcohol."

[9] U.S. Centers for Disease Control, Youth Risk Behavior Survey, quoted in Ellen Flax,

"White Students Twice as Likely As Blacks to Smoke, Study Finds," *Education Week* 11 (September 1991):10.

[10] D. Scott-Jones and A. White, "Correlates of Sexual Activity in Early Adolescence," *Journal of Early Adolescence* 10 (May 1990):221–38; Dryfoos, *Youth at Risk*, chart p. 67.

[11] D. Forrest and S. Singh, "The Sexual and Reproductive Behavior of American Women," *Family Planning Perspectives* 22 (1990):208, Table 4.

[12] C. Irwin and M. Shafer, "Adolescent Sexuality: The Problem of a Negative Outcome of a Normative Behavior," paper prepared for the Cornell University Medical College Conference "Adolescents at Risk: Medical and Social Perspectives," Cornell University, February 1991.

[13] M. Sullivan, *The Male Role in Teenage Pregnancy and Parenting: New Directions for Public Policy* (New York: Vera Institute of Justice, 1990), p. 21.

[14] Irwin and Shafer, "Adolescent Sexuality."

[15] Children's Defense Fund, unpublished paper, Washington, DC, 1991.

[16] K. Moore, *Facts at a Glance* (Washington, DC: Child Trends, 1988). See also K. Moore, "Trends in Teenage Childbearing in the U.S.: 1970–1988" (Los Alamitos, CA: TEC Networks, March 1991).

[17] Irwin and Shafer, "Adolescent Sexuality."

[18] Ibid.

[19] Quoted over the phone by the National AIDS Clearing House from U.S. Centers for Disease Control, *U.S. AIDS Cases Reported in July 1991*, 1991.

[20] L. D'Angelo et al., "HIV Infection in Adolescents: Can We Predict Who Is at Risk?" poster presentation at the Fifth International Conference on AIDS, June 1989.

[21] M. Wolfe, "Women and HIV/AIDS Education," paper prepared for the NEA Health Information Network, Atlanta, 1991.

[22] Ibid.

[23] Ibid.

[24] *The State of Adolescent Health in Minnesota*, Minnesota Youth Health Survey (Minneapolis: Adolescent Health Database Project, February 1989).

[25] H. Reinherz, A. Frost, and B. Pakiz, *Changing Faces: Correlates of Depressive Symptoms in Late Adolescence* (Boston: Simmons College School of Social Work, 1990).

[26] Gans and Blyth, *America's Adolescents*, p. 11.

[27] D. Hawkins, "Risk Focussed Prevention," speech to the Coordinating Council on Juvenile Justice and Delinquency Prevention, 1990; Jessor, "Risk Behavior"; J. Gibbs, *Not Schools Alone* (Sacramento, CA: California Department of Education, 1990); E. Werner, "Vulnerability and Resiliency: The Children of Kauai," paper presented at a conference on Vulnerability and Resiliency in Children and Families, Baltimore, March 1991.

[28] U.S. National Research Council, Panel on Adolescent Pregnancy and Childbearing, C. Hayes, ed., *Risking the Future: Adolescent Sexuality, Pregnancy, and Childbearing* (Washington, DC: National Academy, 1987).

[29] Hayes, *Risking the Future*; D. Kirby, *Sexuality Education: An Evaluation of Programs and Their Effects* (Santa Cruz: Network Publications, 1984); J. Leo, "Sex and Schools," *Time* (November 1986):54–60.

[30] M. Stubbs, *Sex Education and Sex Stereotypes: Theory and Practice*, Working Paper No. 198 (Wellesley, MA: Wellesley College Center for Research on Women, ERIC Document Service No. 306-655, 1989), p. 7.

[31] Ibid., p. 8; M. Rotheram-Borus et al., "Reducing HIV Sexual Risk Behaviors among Runaway Adolescents," *Journal of the American Medical Association* 266 (4 September 1991):1237–41.

[32] M. Eisen, G. Zellman, and A. McAlister, "Evaluating the Impact of a Theory-Based Sexuality and Contraceptive Education

Program," *Family Planning Perspectives* 22 (November/December 1990):261–71; M. Rotheram-Borus et al., "Reducing HIV Sexual Risk Behaviors."

[33] S. Ashton-Warner, *Teacher* (New York: Simon and Schuster, 1963); J. Logan, *Teaching Stories,* paper presented at the American Association of University Women Fellowship, Washington, DC, 1991.

[34] For some disabled girls and women, issues surrounding control and ownership of their own bodies are particularly problematic. For a full discussion of many of these issues see M. Fine and A. Asch, eds., *Women with Disabilities: Essays in Psychology, Culture, and Politics* (Philadelphia, PA: Temple University Press, 1988).

[35] Emily Yoffe, "Girls Who Go Too Far," *Newsweek,* 22 July 1991, pp. 58–59.

[36] J. Martin, *Reclaiming a Conversation: The Ideal of the Educated Woman* (New Haven, CT: Yale University Press, 1985); J. Miller, *Toward a New Psychology of Women* (Boston, MA: Beacon Press, 1976); C. Gilligan, N. Lyons, and T. Hammer, eds., *Making Connections: The Relational Worlds of Adolescent Girls at the Emma Willard School* (Troy, NY: Emma Willard School, 1989); C. Gilligan et al., eds., *Mapping the Moral Domain: A Contribution of Women's Thinking to Psychological Theory and Education* (Cambridge, MA: Harvard University Press, 1988); N. Noddings and P. Shore, *Awakening the Inner Eye: Intuition in Education* (New York: Teachers College Press, 1984); N. Noddings, *Caring: A Feminine Approach to Ethics and Moral Education* (Berkeley, CA: University of California Press, 1984); C. Witherell and N. Noddings, *Stories Lives Tell: Narrative and Dialogue in Education* (New York: Teachers College Press, 1991); M. Belenky et al., *Women's Ways of Knowing: The Development of Self, Voice, and Mind* (New York: Basic Books, 1986); see also P. Elbow, *Writing without Teachers* (London: Oxford University Press, 1973).

[37] A. Kohn, "Caring Kids: The Role of the School," *Phi Delta Kappan* 72 (March 1991):496–506; A. Kohn, "Responding to Others: The Child Development Project," *The Brighter Side of Human Nature* (New York: Basic Books, 1990).

[38] As quoted in *In Their Own Voices: Young Women Talk about Dropping Out,* Project on Equal Education Rights (New York: National Organization for Women Legal Defense and Education Fund, 1988), p. 12.

[39] Ibid.

[40] State of Michigan, Department of Education, Office of Sex Equity in Education, "The Influence of Gender Role Socialization on Student Perceptions," June 1990.

Index

science field, 44-45
Chief state school officers
selection of, 14
women as, 13
Child abuse as evaded issue, 142-43
Classroom curriculum
activities, impact of design of,
124-25
African-American students,
teacher interactions with,
123-24
attention to male students by
teachers, 119-20
bullying behavior by boys, 129-30
comments given to students, bias
in, 120
connected learning defined,
126-27
cooperative learning, 127
cross-gender cooperation, 127-28
evaluation of students, bias in,
122
failure, student attitudes
concerning, 124
learned helplessness in females
resulting from, 122
math classes, 123
science classes, 123
self-confidence loss in females
resulting from, 122
sexual harassment of girls,
129-30
student interactions, 128-31
successful teaching strategies,
125-28
teacher-student interactions,
119-24
videotaping of teachers, 131
College plans for students
gender differences in, 60-61
socioeconomic status as issue,
60-61
Community values as curriculum
issue, 144-45
Contraceptive use as evaded issue,
134, 136-37, 141
Curriculum
AIDS and HIV as evaded issues,

137-38
child abuse as evaded issue,
142-43
classroom as curriculum. See
Classroom curriculum
community values as curriculum
issue, 144
contraceptive use as evaded
issue, 134, 136-37, 141
earning potential, effect on, 7-8
evaded issues, 132-33
expression of feelings as part
of, 142-45
formal curriculum. See Formal
curriculum
generally, 25, 103-4
health issues, 138-42
homosexuality, 141
physical sciences, 25
sex education, inadequacy of,
135-36, 140-42
sexual activity as evaded issue,
134, 136-37
sexually transmitted diseases,
137-38
substance abuse as evaded issue,
133-34
tacit policies, bias of, 145
violence against women as evaded
issue, 144

D

....

Debate clubs, 114
Depression among girls, 139
Dropping out of school
causes of, 83-85
data, lack of, 80
family-related problems as cause
of, 83
gender roles as factor in, 26, 83
generally, 80
High School and Beyond Survey, 81
minorities, rates among, 81
poverty levels related to, 82
repeating grades, effect of, 84
return to school, rates of, 82

statistical methodologies for
measuring, 80-81

E

Eating disorders among girls,
138-39
Eccles, Jacquelynne, 122
Education-reform-report
commissions
female representation on, 10-11
gender equity issues, inclusion
of, 10-11
Emotional development of girls
acceptance by same-sex peers,
importance of, 19
body image as factor, 18, 22,
138-39
body weight as factor, 18
cultural differences in
attitudes, 19, 21
curriculum, effect of, 117-18
depression in adolescence, 19,
22, 139
early-maturing girls, problems
of, 18-19
eating disorders, 138-39
gender role development, effect
on, 17-19
popularity, attitudes toward, 19
racial differences in attitudes,
19, 21
self-esteem levels. See Self-
esteem in girls
suicide among girls, 139-40
transition from elementary to
high school, 21
Employment of women
limitations on job access in, 7
segregation by gender in, 7
wage levels, 7-8
Equal access to education defined,
14
Ethno-cultural background as issue,
11-12
Expression of feelings as

curriculum issue, 142-45
Extracurricular activities
debate clubs, role of, 114
Hispanic girls, participation by,
78
National Education Longitudinal
Survey, findings of, 77
participation in, gender
differences in, 77-79
Title IX requirements, effect of,
77-79

F

Fine, M., 143
Formal curriculum
American Association for the
Advancement of Science, reforms
by, 112
American Indians, representation
of, 117
authors of books in, women as,
107
backlash against women, 110
condescension to girls, 110
cultural inaccuracy, 109
debate clubs, role of, 114
denial of achievements or
authority of women, 110
divide-and-conquer strategies,
110
double standards for sexes, 110
exclusion of girls, 109
gender equity defined, 109-10
gender-fair curriculum defined,
111
history curriculum, reforms of,
112-14
history texts, 108
impact of, 105-6
isolation of materials on girls,
109
math curriculum, reforms of, 111
multicultural readings as part
of, 107-8
mutlicultural debate, 116-17

National Council of Teachers of
Mathematics, reforms by, 111
National Education Association
checklist for bias, 110
New York City schools, reform in,
116-17
nonsexist language in textbooks,
108
out-dated materials, use of,
115-16
purpose of subject areas, 114-15
race equity defined, 109-10
recommendations for change,
151-52
research on, 106-9
resistance to reform, 115
science curriculum, reforms of,
112
social studies, reform of, 116-17
stereotyping of sexes, 109
subordination of girls, 109
superficiality of attention to
social issues, 109
teachers, attitudes of, 111
teacher training reinforcing sex
bias, 107
textbooks, women represented in,
106-8
Frazee, P., 76

G

Gans, J., 137
Garnett, P., 126
Gender role development
body weight as factor, 18
cultural differences in
attitudes, 19, 21
early adolescence, 17-18
early-maturing girls, problems
of, 18-19
elementary school level, 17
generally, 16
menstruation, influence of onset
of, 18
play groups, sex segregation of,
18

popularity, attitudes toward, 19
preschool age, 16
racial differences in attitudes,
19, 21
self-esteem levels, 19
Gilligan, Carol, 20, 114, 144
Goodlad, J., 119
Goodwin, D., 72
Grades, gender differences in
generally, 26, 34
mathematics, 40
science, 42
Greenberg, Selma, 25, 27

H

Harlan, S., 76
Harvard Project on the Psychology
of Women and the Development of
Girls, 20
Harway, M., 16
High School and Beyond Survey,
35-37, 81
Hispanic girls and women
athletic programs, participation
in, 78
drop-out rates for, 81
employment of, 7
family income, contribution to,
7-8
High School and Beyond Survey of
reading skills, 35-36
socioeconomic factors in academic
success, 57-62
wage levels of, 7
History, study of
curriculum, reforms of, 112-14
textbooks, gender bias in, 108-9
Hogue, Dorothy, 63
Homosexuality as evaded issue, 141

I

Income levels for women
African-American families, effect
on, 7-8

education of women, impact of, 8-9
family income, education of women as factor in, 8-9
Hispanic families, effect on, 7-8
men's income levels compared, 7-8
In-service training of educators, 14-15

J

Jacklin, Carol, 35
Johnson, R., 68

K

Kahle, J., 27, 126
Kane, R., 76
Kerber, Linda, 117
Kidder, Tracy, 115
Klein, Susan S., 25, 109
Knowles, T., 149
Kohn, Alfie, 144

L

Language arts
test scores on, 34
Lee, V., 149
Liss, M., 16
Logan, Judy, 142

M

Maccoby, Eleanor, 18, 35
Marks, H., 149
Martin, Jane Roland, 144
Math skills
age of student as factor, 46
attitudes toward subject, gender differences in, 49-50
classroom curriculum, differing experiences of, 45-46
concentrations of students in

math classes, 43
confidence levels, gender differences in, 46-48
curriculum, reforms of, 111
employment opportunities, effect on, 8
gender differences in, 38-40
gender gap, decreases in, 51-52
higher level classes, sex segregation in, 14
international levels of skills, America's standing in, 41
interventions to help girls, 47-48
methodologies for testing, varying results from, 39
methods to encourage, 53-54
problem solving differences between sexes, 94-95
recommendations for reform concerning, 152-53
socioeconomic factors, effect of, 57-58
stereotypical gender roles as factor, 49-50
test scores, 38-40, 93-95
Matthews, Martha, 109
McCune, Shirley, 109
McIntosh, Peggy, 113
Meyer, R., 72
Miller, Jean Baker, 144
Minority groups
African-American girls and women. See African-American girls and women
American Indian education programs, 55
bilingual education programs, 55
drop-out rates for. See Dropping out of school
mutlicultural debate over curriculum, 116-17
school administration, representation in, 13
school boards, as members of, 13
socio-economic status as issue. See Socio-economic status as

35-37
National Assessment of
Educational Progress survey,
35-37
National Education Longitudinal
Survey, 35-36
socioeconomic factors, effect of,
57-58
test scores on, 34
Recommendations for change
administrator training and
evaluation improvements, 150-51
counselor training and evaluation
improvements, 150-51
formal curriculum improvements,
151-52
girls' role in, 154-55
health issues as curriculum
issues, 155-56
mathematics study for girls,
improvements in, 152-53
science study for girls,
improvements in, 152-53
sexuality issues as curriculum
issues, 155-56
teacher training and evaluation
improvements, 150-51
testing and assessment,
improvements in, 154
Title IX enforcement, 150
vocational training, improvements
in, 153-54
Rogers, Annie, 20
Rowe, M., 27, 126

S
....

Sadker, David, 107, 119-20
Sadker, Myra, 107, 119-20
SAT. See Scholastic Achievement
Test (SAT)
Schau, C., 109
Scholastic Achievement Test (SAT)
males favored by, 93-95
math scores, gender differences
in, 40
math test, gender bias in, 93-95

men's college performance,
overpredicting of, 97
predictor of college performance,
as, 97
scholarship discrimination
resulting from, 98
science scores, gender
differences in, 42
sex discrimination resulting
from, 98-99
verbal scores, gender differences
in, 35
verbal test, gender bias in,
92-93
women's college performance,
underpredicting of, 97-98
School administration
minorities in, percentage of, 13
percentage of women in, 13
recommendations for change,
150-51
School boards
minorities as members of, 13
percentage of women on, 13
women as members of, 13
Science, study of
age of student as factor, 46
attitudes toward subject, gender
differences in, 49-50
classroom curriculum, differing
experiences of, 45-46
concentrations of students in
science classes, 43-44
confidence levels, gender
differences in, 46-48
generally, 25
higher level classes, sex
segregation in, 14
increases in gender differences
in, 41-42
interventions to help girls,
47-48
methods to encourage, 53-54
recommendations for reform
concerning, 152-53
test performance, bias in, 99
Scott, K., 109
Self-esteem in girls

curriculum, effect of, 117-18
emotional development, as part
of, 19-22
Sex education, inadequacy of,
135-36, 140-42, 155-56
Sexual activity as evaded issue,
134, 136-37
Sexual harassment of girls, 129-30
Sexually transmitted diseases as
evaded issue, 137-38
Smith, R., 149
Sobol, Thomas, 116
Socioeconomic status as issue
achievement levels related to, 55
government-funded programs, lack
of information from, 55
math scores, effect on, 57-58
motivation of students, 60
National Coalition of Advocates
for Students, study by, 11-12
National Education Longitudinal
Survey, results of, 56-62
predictor of academic success,
as, 56-58
reading scores, effect on, 57-58
Spatial skills, gender differences
in, 41
Special education
gender inequity in, 29-31
selection for, gender bias in,
29-31
Sports programs. See Athletic
programs
Standardized tests. See Testing,
gender bias in
Stanford Binet test, 92
State education agencies
women as heads of, 14
Stein, Nan, 130
Steinberg, R., 76
Stubbs, Margaret, 130
Students at risk
National Coalition of Advocates
for Students, study by, 11-12
Style, Emily, 110
Substance abuse as evaded issue,
133-34
Suicide among girls, 139-40

T

Teaching profession
attention to male students by
teachers, 119-20
bullying behavior by boys,
attitudes concerning, 129-30
comments given to students, bias
in, 120
harassment of girls, attitudes
concerning, 129-30
nontraditional courses, sexual
harassment by teachers in, 76
percentage of women in, 13
recommendations for change in
training, 150-51
successful teaching strategies,
125-28
teacher training reinforcing sex
bias, 107
videotaping of teachers, 131
vocational education, gender
stereotyping of teachers in,
74-75
Teen fathers, 68-69
Teen pregnancy and motherhood
community programs for, effect
of, 69-71
contributing factors to, 65-66
costs to public, 64
discrimination related to, 26
fathers, teens as, 68-69
generally, 63
high school diploma received,
figures on, 70
incidents of births to
adolescents, 63-64
school response to, 67
self-image as factor, 65-66
sex-role stereotyping as factor,
65-66
Testing, gender bias in
American College Testing Program
(ACT), 98
anxiety levels, 97
California Achievement Test
(CAT), 92

completion of tests, 96
examples of bias, 91
gender references on tests,
  incidence of, 91-92
generally, 89
impact of findings, 97
inaccuracies resulting from, 99
math testing, 93-95
observers of test performance,
  bias of, 99
portrayals of sexes in reading
  comprehension tests, 91-92
question types as factor, 96
recommendations for reform, 154
reliability of tests, 90
SAT test, 92-95
science inquiry items, 96-97
Stanford Binet test, 92
test results as reflections of
  current conditions, 90
validity of tests, 90-91
Test scores, gender differences in
  generally, 26, 34
  mathematics skills, 38-40
  reading skills, 35-37
  Scholastic Achievement Test. See
    Scholastic Achievement Test
    (SAT)
  Spatial skills, 41
  writing skills, 38
Textbooks, gender bias in, 106-9
Tipton, Betty, 121
Title IX of Education Amendment of
  1972
  athletic programs, requirements
    for, 77-79
  enforcement of, 12, 15, 150
  extracurricular activities,
    applicability to, 77-79
  importance of, 12
Tobin, K., 126

V

Verbal skills
  gender differences in, 34-35
  Scholastic Achievement Test
    scores, 35

test scores on, 34
Vetter, L., 76
Violence against women as
  curriculum issue, 144
Vocational education
  Carl C. Perkins Vocational
    Education Act of 1984, 1990
    amendments to, 76-77
  discriminatory employment
    practices, effect of, 73
  earning power, effect on, 72-73
  funding for sex-equity in, lack
    of, 73-74
  generally, 72
  goals for, 76-77
  legislation, reform in, 76-77
  minorities, enrollment by, 73
  National Assessment of Vocational
    Education, findings of, 73-74
  nontraditional courses, sexual
    harassment in, 76
  recommendations for reform,
    153-54
  reform of, 75-76
  sex-equity grants for, lack of,
    73-74
  sex-stereotyped occupations,
    distribution of women in, 76
  teachers gender stereotyping of,
    74-75

W

Wage levels for women. See Income
  levels for women
Warner, Sylvia Ashton, 142
Wilbur, Gretchen, 111-12
Witt, J., 72
Wood, George H., 3
Writing skills
  test scores for, 38

Z

Zane, N., 143
Zieky, M., 97
  findings of, 73-74

RESOURCES

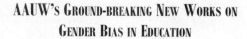

AAUW's Ground-breaking New Works on Gender Bias in Education

Schoolgirls: Young Women, Self-Esteem, and the Confidence Gap
(Doubleday, 1994)
Riveting book by journalist Peggy Orenstein in association with AAUW shows how girls in two racially and economically diverse California schools suffer the loss of self-esteem documented in *Shortchanging Girls, Shortchanging America*. 384 pages. $18.95 AAUW members/$21.95 nonmembers.

Hostile Hallways: The AAUW Survey on Sexual Harassment in America's Schools
The first national study of sexual harassment in school, based on the experiences of 1,632 students in grades 8 through 11. Gender and ethnic/racial (African American, Hispanic, and white) data breakdowns included. Commissioned by the AAUW Educational Foundation and conducted by Louis Harris and Associates. 28 pages/1993. $8.95 AAUW members/$11.95 nonmembers.

How Schools Shortchange Girls —The AAUW Report
(Marlowe, 1995)
Disturbing report documents girls' second-class treatment in America's schools, grades K–12. The research report, commissioned by the AAUW Educational Foundation and prepared by the Wellesley College Center for

Research on Women, includes policy recommendations and strategies for change. 240 pages. $11.95 AAUW members/$12.95 nonmembers.

The AAUW Report Executive Summary
Overview of **The AAUW Report** research, with recommendations for educators and policymakers. 8 pages/1992. $6.95 AAUW members/ $8.95 nonmembers.

The AAUW Report Action Guide
Strategies for combating gender bias in school, based on **The AAUW Report** recommendations. 8 pages/1992. $6.95 AAUW members/ $8.95 nonmembers.

Action Alert
AAUW's monthly newsletter monitoring congressional action on educational equity as well as reproductive choice, sexual harassment, and other vital issues. One-year subscription: $20 AAUW members/$25 nonmembers.

Shortchanging Girls, Shortchanging America
Highly readable executive summary of the 1991 poll that awakened the nation to the problem of gender bias in America's schools. Poll shows graphically how classroom gender bias hurts girls' self-esteem, school achievement, and career aspirations. Revised edition, with updated account

of poll's impact and review of school, community, and government action strategies, highlights survey results with charts and graphs. 20 pages/1994. $8.95 AAUW members/ $11.95 nonmembers.

Full Data Report: Shortchanging Girls, Shortchanging America
Complete data on AAUW's 1991 national poll on girls and self-esteem, with survey questions and responses, and banners displaying cross-tabulations. Includes floppy disk with all data. 500 pages/1991. $60 AAUW members/$85 nonmembers.

To order, call 202/785-7761.

Video: Girls Can!
The video complement to *Shortchanging Girls, Shortchanging America*. An inspirational look at programs around the country that are making a difference in fighting gender bias in schools. VHS format. $19.95 AAUW members/ $24.95 nonmembers.

AAUW Issue Briefs
Package of five briefs, with strategies for change: Equitable Treatment of Girls and Boys in the Classroom; Restructuring Education; Stalled Agenda—Gender Equity and the Training of Educators; College Admission Tests: Opportunities or Roadblocks?; Creating a Gender-Fair Multicultural Curriculum. 1990-93. $7.95 AAUW members/$9.95 nonmembers.

....

Help Make a Difference for Today's Girls... and Tomorrow's Leaders

Become part of the American Association of University Women, representing 150,000 college graduates, and help promote education and equity for women and girls. You can add your voice as a Member-at-Large or work on critical issues in one of AAUW's 1,750 local branches. For further membership information, write: AAUW Membership, Dept. U, 1111 Sixteenth Street N.W., Washington, DC 20036-4873, or call 800/326-AAUW, ext. 130.

The AAUW Educational Foundation, a not-for-profit 501(c)(3) organization, provides funds to advance education, research, and self-development for women, and to foster equity and positive societal change. Your dollars support research, community action projects, fellowships for women, and teachers. Send contributions to: AAUW Educational Foundation, Dept. 321, 1111 Sixteenth Street N.W., Washington, DC 20036-4873.

AAUW Resources Order Form

♦

Item	Circle Price Member/Nonmember	Quantity	Total
Schoolgirls	$18.95/$21.95	_____	_____
Hostile Hallways	$8.95/$11.95	_____	_____
How Schools Shortchange Girls	$11.95/$12.95	_____	_____
AAUW Report Summary	$6.95/$8.95	_____	_____
AAUW Report Action Guide	$6.95/$8.95	_____	_____
Action Alert	$20/$25 per year	_____	_____
Shortchanging Girls: Summary	$8.95/$11.95	_____	_____
Girls Can!: Video	$19.95/$24.95	_____	_____
AAUW Issue Briefs 5-Pack	$7.95/$9.95	_____	_____

*For bulk pricing on orders of 10 or more,
call 800/225-9998, ext. 321.*

Subtotal: _____

6% sales tax _____
*(DC, FL
residents only)*

Shipping/
Handling: $4.00

AAUW Membership $35   _____

Total Order: _____

**Please make check or money order payable to AAUW. Do not send cash.
Credit cards are accepted for orders of $10 or more.**

☐ MasterCard   ☐ Visa

Card #__ __ __ __ - __ __ __ __ - __ __ __ __ - __ __ __ __   Expiration _____

Name on card _____

Cardholder signature _____

☐ Please send me information on joining an AAUW branch in my area
(dues vary by branch).

☐ I'd like to join as a Member-at-Large. Enclosed is $35.

**FOR MAIL ORDERS, SEND THIS
FORM TO:**
AAUW Sales Office Dept. 321
P.O. Box 251
Annapolis Junction, MD 20701-0251

FOR TELEPHONE ORDERS, CALL:
800/225-9998, ext. 321